THE END OF TIME

THE END OF TIME

DAVID HOROWITZ

ENCOUNTER BOOKS
SAN FRANCISCO

First edition published in 2005 by Encounter Books, an activity
of Encounter for Culture and Education, Inc., a nonprofit, tax
exempt corporation.

Encounter Books website address: www.encounterbooks.com

Manufactured in the United States and printed on acid-free
paper.

The paper used in this publication meets the minimum require-
ments of ANSI/NISO

Z39.48-1992 (R 1997)(*Permanence of Paper*).

FIRST EDITION

Library of Congress Cataloging-in-Publication Data

Horowitz, David, 1939–.
  The end of time / David Horowitz.
    p.   cm.
  ISBN 1-59403-080-4 (alk. paper)
    1. Horowitz, David, 1939–.   2. Horowitz, David, 1939–
—Health.   3. Horowitz, David, 1939– —Family.
4. Death—Psychological aspects.   5. Death—Moral and
ethical aspects.   6. Cancer—Patients—United States—
Biography.   7. Political activists—United States—
Biography.   I. Title.
E840.8.H67 A3   2005
973.92'092-B22   2005040682

10 9 8 7 6 5 4 3 2 1

It is better to go to the house of mourning than the house of feasting, for that is the end of all; and the living will lay it to his heart.
    —*Ecclesiastes*

Contents

ONE
Going Home

WHEN HE WAS ALIVE AND I WAS STILL YOUNG, my father told me his version of the Fall. "We begin to die the day we are born," he said. What I think my father meant by this was that the cells, which are the invisible elements of our being, are constantly churning in nature's cycle. Silently, without our being aware of their agony, they are inexorably aging and taking us with them. Year by year, the skin parches, the sinews slacken, and the bones go brittle, until one day the process stops, and we are gone.

At least that is what I think my father said because that is all that I can remember. And what I can remember is all that is left of the time we spent together long ago, a fading image now like the rest. I can still see the sunlight on the green hedge where we paused on the sidewalk. I can see the mottled sycamores shading the street, and the way my father turned until the tan dome of his forehead caught the glint of the light when he shared his thought.

We were taking a Saturday walk through the neighborhood. In the yards, the spring warmth had pushed
the yellow daffodils and purple crocuses through the
black earth, creating little splashes of color. I remember the feeling of pleasure I had, and always did, being
alone with him. Or maybe it is the lingering memory
that is the pleasure. I can no longer tell.

When he didn't go to work, my father took walks
every day of his life that I recall. It was only years afterward that it occurred to me that for him the aim of
these walks was not to go somewhere, but to get away.
As though the life he had been given was less than the
one he wanted, or more than one he could bear.

As my father imparted his reflection, the timbre in
his voice gave off no hint of gloom but was detached
and clinical, as though he were making a scientific
observation devoid of human reference. Even now, I
cannot guess what his intentions were, or why he
decided to share this dark insight with me when I was
so innocent of life myself. But he did; and the words
have stuck ever since and into the present, when age is
already on me and has sunk its teeth into my marrow,
and feelings of mortality have made themselves as familiar as hello and goodbye.

It is more than half a century since my father and I took our walk in Sunnyside Gardens. From that time until his death nearly forty years later in the same red-brick row house on the same tree-lined street, we never discussed the subject again. Though I never forgot what he said, I never bothered in all that time to inquire of anyone who might actually know whether it was based on a biological truth, or not. Nor did it ever occur to me that his words might not actually have referred to the objective world, but to his feelings about himself.

My father was a small, well-intentioned man of melancholy humors and roiling regrets. Bleak thoughts enveloped him in a cloud so dense he was rarely able to see the sun behind it. One effect of this rough-weather approach was to make it difficult for him to find pleasure in the opportunities life offered. When good fortune came knocking at his door, he received it more often than not as he would a visitor to the wrong address.

All our days together I wrestled with my father's discontent and tried as best I could to overcome it. But eventually I understood that the well from which he drew his unhappiness was bottomless, and no one could stem its flow. As a result, the lesson he left me was not contained in the earnest lectures he gave, but in the instruction of a life that clung to its defeats like an infant to its mother's breast.

Unlike my father, I do not feel that life is a down-hill run. Nor do I think of it as an arc that rises steadily until it reaches its apogee, tapers, and arches back to earth. The fate we choose is inscribed in multiple flights. Some follow the gravity of rise and fall, while others—those of the spirit for example—may never head down-ward, but climb steadily to the end, where they just drop cliff-like into the dark.

Consequently, there is no right time for last words, no point of demarcation for our *adieux*. There is no designated moment to set down the summary thoughts of a mind still counting. Whether you begin to die at the beginning—as my father believed—or whether you burn brightly to the end, you can't wait forever to pass to others what you have learned. When the time approaches you could already have a foot in oblivion, or be crippled by a stroke, or so blasted with pain as to lose the ability to reflect at all.

In this life, they can haul you off without warning. You can step onto the wrong plane, or off the wrong curb, or into the wrong conversation and be gone. A microorganism can stumble into a passage to your heart and douse the lights before you even learn its name. Or the cells of your being—those busy dying since you were born—can go berserk and betray you, metasta-sizing into a cancer that chokes your last thought. No matter how young you are or how far you get, you can never know if there will be hours enough to finish the page.

Some of us get yanked before our time, while others hang on longer than they should. Still others take themselves out when they think they've had enough. But what is enough, particularly if you wise up to master the game? It doesn't matter. The clock is ticking and the buzzer is set.

This is an injustice that no reformer can repair and no court can redress.

When I began these pages I was living in a Mediterranean-style house perched like an eyrie on the palisades high above the Pacific Ocean. I had gravitated to this refuge only two years before in what I realized was an *homage* to the passion I inherited from my father. It was the only one he ever really allowed himself—his unfulfilled longing for the sea.

On crystal days, which were many, I would look out through picture windows to my only horizon, a panorama of whitecaps and blue water, and miss him. In such moments, my father's ghost would sometimes return to haunt me. I could see the face I had both loved and feared approach on the ether of memory until it was only a breath away. An impulse to please would swell like an ocean wave inside me, and I would look out on the roll of dolphins and pelicans, and welcome my lost father to a luxury neither of us could ever have imagined would be ours.

In these reveries his spirit was so palpable I could almost touch it. I would point my fingers toward the apparition and run them down the slope of its brow until I had fully mapped the frown of his rejection. For there was never a chance he would accept my gift or take its pleasures. Not now; not then; not ever. The opportunity rolled away from us like the ebb of an evening tide. It hardly matters why. Whether he felt he didn't deserve this happiness, or I didn't, or both. It only matters that it was so. In my father's house there were no mansions.

Because he was unable to get what he wanted in this life, my father frittered away his days in dreams of the next. The metaphor of this longing was the sea, limitless and unattainable. What my father desperately wanted—or so he believed—was a world better than the one he had been given. This was the unrequited romance of his life, the object of time only prayers he ever allowed himself. But the world did not heed his prayers. It ignored him, as it does us all, and went its own way.

In the end, my father's disappointment was the gift he gave me, an irony that still connects us beyond the grave. His melancholy taught me the lesson he was unable to learn himself. Don't bury the life you have been given in this world in fantasies of the next; don't betray yourself with impossible dreams.

Are these judgments too harsh? Are they gripes of an ungrateful son? Perhaps the father I think I know was not so helpless after all; perhaps he was even shrewd. Maybe when he shared his thoughts with me on our neighborhood walk, he meant something else entirely. Maybe what he was saying to his son was this: Prepare now for the end.

When the novelist Saul Bellow reached the age of seventy-eight his brain was still kicking like that of a young man. *All Marbles Still Accounted For* is the witty title he devised for a novel he was writing that was still unfinished. In the pages of the books he did send to press, he showed that he was still capable of turning out clever prose and was a step ahead of everyone else in getting things to add up. He remained a master of the game.

In that year Bellow published an elegiac tale about his dying mother, who had been stricken with cancer a lifetime before. The story recounted an embarrassing incident, which its fictional narrator claimed had distracted him from his filial debt. It happened to him on a winter's day, when his mother lay on a bed of pain, gulping the arduous breaths her family knew would be her last.

While his mother suffered, life continued for everyone else, including her son, who went about his job delivering flowers for a local merchant. Late in the afternoon, he was bearing an armful of lilies to the wake of a young girl no older than himself. Entering the room where her coffin lay open, he cast a diffident eye on the lifeless form. After navigating the crowd of mourners and locating the grieving mother, he pressed his funeral bouquet into her arms and fled.

This encounter with death so affected the young man that instead of returning to the shop for more orders or going home, he decided to stop at a nearby office building where his uncle worked. The uncle was out, but as the youth made his way down the hall he passed the open door of a doctor's office and had a chance encounter with a sexual mystery woman. She was lying on a table naked, but failed to react when she caught sight of him spying on her. This seductive behavior planted the idea in his head that she was available for his pleasure. Hot with desire, he allowed her to lure him across town to an apartment, where she induced him to undress.

All the while, his flesh was burning, which caused his brain cells to go numb so he didn't see what was coming. When he had completely removed his clothes, the hooker grabbed them and fled into the bitter cold of the Chicago night. Ruefully, Bellow's narrator recalls how he put on a dress that he found in a closet and went out into the freezing air, dreading the humiliation that awaited him and his father's anger when he got back.

His money was gone and he had no carfare, so he went into a local bar, where his luck improved when the bartender paid him to see a drunken customer home. Afterward, he boarded the El that would take him home as well. Sitting in the train car, alone with his shame, he had an unnerving thought. Until then, he had been afraid of facing his father's wrath at what he had done. But now he began to hope for the anger instead. For he remembered what his desire had caused him to forget. His mother was dying. If his father was angry at him when he stepped through the front door, he would know she was still alive.

One lesson of this story concerns animal desire. Sex is a force so powerful that it is the source of endless human embarrassment and considerable personal grief. Lust will frustrate a man's best efforts to elevate himself and make of his life something dignified and worthy. It will induce him to do things that are stupid and humbling. Like shaming our mothers on their deathbeds.

Yet desire is only a subtheme of Bellow's tale, which recalls facts taken from his own life. Bellow's fictional narrator dedicates his memoir to his son as a memento for when he is gone, calling it, *Something to Remember Me By.* This is a typical Bellow trope, since it is a story that anyone would prefer to forget. Perhaps this is why it took Bellow until his seventy-eighth year to write it down.

The main theme of this memoir is announced in its opening paragraph, which is constructed around the image of a turntable. The author doesn't identify the turntable he has in mind, nor does he make clear whether it is the kind one finds in children's playgrounds or the kind used to play vinyl records and produce musical sounds, gone now like so much else. Instead he writes, "When there is too much going on, more than you can bear, you may choose to assume that nothing in particular is happening, that your life is going round and round like a turntable." Perhaps the denial he is referring to is larger than the moment itself. Perhaps he is hinting that the music of your days can lull you into an illusion that the present will go on and on, and will never go anywhere else. Or perhaps, more simply, that your life is in motion when you think you are just standing still.

Until something happens, that is. Until you get clobbered by an event and wake up to the fact that the stillness is an illusion. That everything is changing about you, and that one day it will come to an end.

In Bellow's case the clobbering was his mother's death. Inexplicably and without warning, the cells in her body had run amok and created a malignancy in her breast. Soon, it was choking her, until she was gasping for air and spitting up blood. And then she was gone.

When Bellow's mother had breathed her last and her agonies finally came to an end, the coroner did not know what age to put on the certificate of death. Like many immigrants she had no idea of the date she was born and neither did anyone else. So the coroner did what he could and put on the certificate what he saw. She seemed to be a woman of "about fifty," he wrote. The certificate was like a tag on ancient bones that had been exhumed in an archaeological dig and that no one could identify. Her surviving son was only seventeen.

"One day you are aware that what you took to be a turntable, smooth, flat and even, was in fact a whirlpool, a vortex," Bellow observed. The vortex of his mother's death had sucked some part of him beneath the surface and it never came back. "My life was never the same after my mother died," he said long after the event and in another context. In the story, he wrote: "I knew she was dying, and didn't allow myself to think about it—there's your turntable."

In the business of mothers dying, fate dealt me a better hand than it did Saul Bellow. My mother lived to a ripe age and was vigorous to the end. When she had her first stroke my children were already adults, and had given me two grandchildren besides. I was well into the cycle of the generations. This prepared me in a way that the young Bellow could not have been for the cold hand of mortality that a parent's death lays on your heart. When the time arrived for my mother to go, it seemed almost natural that her life should draw to a conclusion. Even though her death was sudden and unannounced, I had time enough to prepare for it, to see the vortex coming.

On the other hand, the months before she died were not unlike the day remembered in Bellow's story. I, too, let myself go round like a turntable, running about the business of my life while the clock on hers ticked mercilessly away. What else could I have done? Can one focus on death like a watched pot, waiting for it to boil? If we concentrated on our dying with an intensity that never let up, everything in our lives would come to a stop, until our days would seem like the grave itself. So instead, we don't pay attention to where we are headed but go round on the turntable and pretend we are standing still.

Here's a tip. As you go spinning round, turn one eye to the side every now and then. Look over the edge and focus on a fixed object. Find a way to calculate your progress. Otherwise, life will pass you by before you wake up.

My father—may his memory be blessed—was right: Never forget the cells that are dying. Life is not a turntable, and one day the music will stop.

When I think of Saul Bellow's unhappy evening years ago, I am prompted to consider how different we are, and how incommensurable the lives we are given. How, as a result, each of us is an impenetrable enigma to the other: the young Bellow to the mystery woman who made off with his clothes; the mystery woman to him; both to us.

What would it do to your sense of things if your mother had died a cruel and punishing death when you were still a youth of seventeen? How would the memory of this loss affect your optimism, your sense of threat in the environment around you? Would it cause you to become a man more quickly? Or would the missing parent make it more difficult to grow up at all? Losing one's mother at such a youthful age could certainly make the world seem a lonelier and more unforgiving place.

Saul Bellow eventually married five women. Several of his biographers claim to have found a pattern in his choice of wives, identifying them as motherly types. This includes even the last, who was forty years his junior and took care of him in old age. Are these really psychological insights into Bellow's inner life, or merely critical sour grapes? Who can read another's heart?

Our origins create a gravity that controls our ends but also leaves us to our own devices. In every family there is one who has gone this way, while another heads somewhere else. This one surrenders to awful circumstances; that one survives the worst and flourishes. One benefits from benign conditions; another rejects them. This tells us that we have a biblical free will and are finally the gods of what we become.

Bellow's story may not seem so hard when viewed from others' perspectives. When my friend Christopher Hitchens was twenty-three and living in London, he got a call from one of his friends. The morning paper was reporting that someone with his mother's name had been murdered by her lover in an Athens hotel. "So I went out and got the paper and there it was," he remembers. He called the Athens police and boarded a plane and was led to the apartment where the tragedy had taken place. At first, the police deemed it a murder because there was blood everywhere. But then they found a suicide note addressed to Christopher that said, "You will understand one day."

Would he? If you're not in Christopher's shoes, it's hard to imagine how this primal scene would not work itself into the inner ear of the soul and tip the balance of a life. Christopher said, "That was sort of the end of family life, really." What does this statement mean to him? We cannot know, any more than we can know the meaning of his mother's final note. What we know is that the individual soul is life's impenetrable mystery: No matter how intense the intimacies we share, no matter how common our humanity, its code cannot be cracked. This creates a silence between every one of us that is as deep and as wide as the ocean floor.

When he was eighty-five and nearing his end, Saul Bellow published another fiction called *Ravelstein*, which is about the death of his friend, the critic Allan Bloom. Toward the story's end, the narrator goes on a Caribbean vacation with his younger wife, and becomes deathly ill from food poisoning. This is like something that happened to Bellow himself.

In his fevers, the narrator has a vision of a past conversation about death with Ravelstein, now gone. "When I said that the pictures would stop he reflected seriously on my answer, came to a full stop, and considered what I might mean by this. No one can give up on the pictures." Even as Bellow puts these words on the page, however, he does not seem wholly convinced by Ravelstein's claim. "The pictures might, yes they *might* continue," the narrator replies. "I wonder if anyone believes that the grave is all there is." Impatient with this wavering, Ravelstein insists, "No one can give up on the pictures. The pictures must and will continue."

Half a page later Bellow returns to the thought: "This is the involuntary and normal, the secret, esoteric, confidence of the man of flesh and blood. The flesh would shrink and go, the blood would dry, but no one believes in his mind of minds or heart of hearts that the pictures *do* stop."

What else would you expect from a creator of images? Would a lifetime of lonely labors be requited if all that authorial effort crumbled to dust with the pages that recorded it and vanished? Art is long and life is short and the technology of preservation is relentlessly advancing. Memories and thoughts were once recorded on parchments that decayed over decades. Now we can put our writings in vacuum-sealed time capsules that will last for centuries. But in the eye of eternity, this posterity is nothing. Can anybody believe that human artifice will actually outrun time itself?

It is more plausible that the images come to an end. *All* the images: The images Bloom impressed on others when he was still alive; Bloom's images of them; and the image of Bloom in the figure of Ravelstein so skillfully drawn by his friend. Eventually the vapors of time will dissolve them, and they will disappear into the black hole from which they came. The pictures will stop.

Think of death as a horizon that travels with us, until one day we reach it, and it becomes us. We vanish in an eye-blink, leaving behind only a little vacancy, like the wake of a ship that is lost at sea. Of all the pictures in our minds, this is the one that is hardest to focus. Yet, it is the one that tells us who we are.

Do even the brave souls among us who can look coldly on their exits believe in their hearts that they will disappear? Or do they secretly hope to wake on the other side of the horizon in a place that feels like home?

As an agnostic, I do not actually know whether the pictures stop any more than the faithful know that they don't. This uncertainty about our end is the one fact that links us more than any other. Pitiful ignorance about what matters most is the humility that unites us, doubters and believers alike. This is our humanity: Not to know who we are or what we will become.

I don't believe the pictures continue. Would it be a good idea if they did? Do believers imagine that the immortal soul still *feels* after the vessel is shattered? Can we still love and hate and have regrets beyond the grave? Consider what kind of hell eternity would be like if we had to look forever on the poor lives we have left behind. Or if we had to face ourselves knowing how the story ends without the power to make it different. Do we really want eternity to think about what we have done and how we have failed? Or does God make it all up to us when we are dead, so that we are forgiven, and forgive others, and forget?

What are "intimations of immortality" but feelings that we *must* live on, that we need the pictures to continue? Yet such intimations cannot be so easily dismissed, since feelings themselves are often about things that are hidden and also true. We rely on them as instincts because they are more "in the body" than abstract thoughts, therefore closer to what is real, to earth. The word "sense" expresses this intimacy between feeling and knowledge. When we "sense" something to be true, we mean it has touched us even if we cannot articulate just how. To know through feeling is to know in the heart.

As an agnostic, I have no idea if the universe began with a bang or has existed forever, or is the work of a Creator. But regarding what I do know, I am convinced that the biblical book of Genesis conveys a central truth about human fate.

The First Parents wanted to be like God and could not be satisfied with anything else. Though they were immortal and lived without labor and suffered no pain, earthly abundance was insufficient for them. Even in Eden they felt denied; paradise was not enough. What they lacked became their want. "What is good without evil [they asked in effect] or love without hate?" Perverse though it may be, this logic made sense. For what can be desired that cannot be withheld? We are defined by negatives; they describe the emptiness we fill.

God warned Adam and Eve that death would be the reward for their immodest desire. But they rejected His warning and pursued their ambition anyway, and were punished.

This account in Genesis is the story of our beginning and our end. We are creatures of desires that cannot be satisfied and of dreams that will not come true.

Man's longing for God can be understood as the need to be released from the pain of being human, even if that pain is paradise itself. To live eternally in paradise without knowledge of what we lacked, even if it was knowledge of evil, even if it *was* evil, was unhappiness to us. To end our unhappiness, we chose to die.

On a shelf in my living room is a rotogravure portrait featuring a spirited teenager in a nineteenth-century frock, brashly showing her skirt. This is my grandmother Rose, who was still a young woman when I was born, and had a fatal stroke when I was in my twenties. Other than this photograph I have no idea what the girl in the picture was like. In my kitchen there is an incomplete set of her wedding crystal and a blue teapot bearing her initials in silver and the year of her marriage, 1898. These are all the pieces of her life that are left except for a few fading images in the memories of a handful of people who soon will be gone.

A quarter of a century after my grandmother's death, my mother, who had inherited her high blood pressure, suffered a series of smaller strokes. The strokes did not kill her at first, but damaged an important function in her brain. Afterward, she was still in good physical shape, but could barely remember who she was.

Somewhere in the black hole that her memory had become, she had even misplaced my father and could no longer retrieve him. Although they had been married for more than fifty years, the life she had lived with him had slipped into the ether and she could not recognize his name. The images of my grandmother's life were fading in other heads; my mother's had disappeared in her own. All she could remember was the house on Maple Street in New Haven where she grew up and the one in Sunnyside where I did.

Because the strokes left her unable to take care of herself, I returned to the Sunnyside row house where she still lived and moved her to my home in Los Angeles. This was an English Tudor with a redwood in the front yard, which offered her more comforts than she had ever known. Though it was a good life for her, she was unhappy. She desired what she lacked. She wanted to go back to the home she remembered and had lost.

My mother could not adjust to the fact that she had become as helpless as a child, and was being taken care of by her son. Her persistent melancholy prompted me to search for another home for her, where she would not feel like a burden whom time was passing by. I located a retirement center where she would be surrounded by people her own age, most of whom were even more helpless than she was. Although I had qualms about moving her to an alien place, she seemed happier there from the day she arrived. The diminished lives she encountered in her new setting made her feel more in control and less aware of what she had lost. But even though it was called a "home," the people she lived with had no idea who she was.

The book of Psalms says that all flesh is grass and that each of us is like a flower in the field that flourishes and dies: "The wind passes over it, and it is gone, and its place knows it no more." Our feeling that we have a place in the world is a deception we practice on ourselves, because we have none. It is this pretense that makes an otherwise unendurable existence bearable and at times even happy. There is really no place in the world that "knows" us in the Psalmist's sense. There is only an illusion sustained by others who love us, and who, like us, will soon be gone.

But the feeling is so strong that the reality does not matter. The illusion of home will overcome even the most grotesque scenes of family dysfunction. We can be battered by a spouse and never want to leave. We can spend our childhood in a household of abuse and fear, but as long as we draw breath our hearts will still want to go home. On this earth our comfort is deception and we can never tell whether we are dreaming, or not.

Sometimes in the night, I wake up with an image of my terrified mother in her last moments on earth. It is only an image but to me it is as painful as if it were real. The source of my nightmare is the fact that when the time came for her to go I was not there to help her. Three years earlier I had left the Tudor house, moving twice before settling alone in a tower of apartments in the Los Angeles marina. It was one of more than twenty addresses I have called home. The apartment was only a short drive from the hospital where my mother lay dying, but by the time someone called me and I was able to reach her, she was already gone.

It was this phone call that planted in my mind the suffering image that wakes me in the night. The manager of the home was on the phone telling me how my mother had started out of her sleep and summoned one of the strangers to come to her bedside. When the stranger came, my mother said, "Something is terribly wrong," as though what was wrong might not be happening to her. It was the impersonal voice my mother had used her whole life to avoid what appeared to be embarrassments to self. The Angel of Death had come for her, but she called for help in a way that would not draw unnecessary attention to the one who was in need. This is the painful image that harrows my sleep and leaves me with feelings of helplessness and despair. When these nightmares come, I comfort myself with the thought that had I reached her in time, it would only have been to see her off to where I could not follow her, to the horizon each of us must meet alone.

Arriving at the Cedars-Sinai hospital complex, I entered the room where my mother lay on her gurney and where death had already transfigured her. The corpse was twisted in a tangle of medical tubes, bruised and discolored by the doctors' attempts to bring her back. The figure in front of me was no longer my mother, and I fled into the night to be alone with my loss. In the hospital courtyard, under a luminous black sky, I was enveloped in a wave of feeling that seemed to issue from the night itself. For a moment I was comforted and at peace. And then the wave receded, leaving me to myself again.

In the weeks prior to these events, I was busy with my own life and frequently out of town. On the turntable, as Bellow would have said. Even though my mother's mind was no longer right, I knew that in her heart she was missing me. And I was missing her. But I couldn't get myself off the turntable to see her. Until a day came when despite my busyness, or perhaps because of it, I made a point of taking time out to stop by and visit her. There was no way I could have known that this would be her last day on earth.

I drove to the retirement home and came upon her in the common room, where she was waiting. It was early morning and I took a chair beside her. We sat together in the rays of muffled light pouring through the aged curtains and reflected in filaments of microscopic dust, and held each other's hands. I was happy and completely at peace; and I believe she was too. It was as intimate and satisfying as any moment I had ever shared with her.

After she was gone, I thought about her passage and the gratitude I felt for the time with her, and asked myself, *Why was I there? How had I come to her the very morning that was her last?* I have no answer.

More than 350 years ago, in the city of Paris, the scientist Blaise Pascal was deathly ill and approaching his horizon. He was still a young man and though wracked with pain was busily taking notes on scraps of paper for what would be his final work. The scraps had been cut with scissors and sewn together with needle and thread. They were found after his death in a disordered state. No one knew how they were to be put together. The plan for ordering them was still in Pascal's mind, which was now out of anyone's reach. The little notebooks he had left behind contained the thoughts he had been unable to complete before the end.

When he was gone it remained for others to put the scraps in order and identify them with numbers and provide the collection with a name. They called the result Pascal's *Pensées:* "The Thoughts of Monsieur Pascal about Religion and Other Matters, Which Were Discovered among His Papers after He Died."

Number 205 of the scraps that Pascal left contains this famous cry: "When I consider the short duration of my life, swallowed up in the eternity before and after, the space which I fill, and even can see, engulfed in the infinite immensity of spaces of which I am ignorant and which know me not, I am frightened and aston-ished at being here rather than there; for there is no reason why here rather than there, why now rather than then. Who has put me here?"

It is the unanswered question of every soul in the night surrounding it. We can never know who is the master of this house, or whether it has a master at all. Or who has put us here, or where we are going.

Pascal was one of the greatest scientific minds that ever lived. Yet, he looked into the eye of the universe and could not find an answer. Without a Creator to make sense of it, Pascal wrote, a human life is "intolerable."

So what are we to do? Although Pascal was able to unlock the mysteries of the physical universe better than almost any man who ever lived, and although he solved mathematical puzzles for all time, it is his attempt to answer this question that we most remember him by.

As a mathematician, Pascal invented the world's first calculator and was a pioneer of probability the-ory. Using this theory, he devised formulas for winning games of chance that are still employed today. It was only natural that he should attempt to analyze the spiritual uncertainties that surround us in the same clinical way he went about his scientific studies.

"229. This is what I see and what troubles me. I look on all sides, and I see only darkness everywhere. Nature presents to me nothing, which is not a matter of doubt and concern. If I saw nothing there that revealed a Divinity, I would come to a negative conclusion; if I saw everywhere the signs of a Creator, I would remain peacefully in faith. But seeing too much to deny and too little to be sure, I am in a state to be pitied; ...."

The sadness of our condition runs like an Aeolian theme through Pascal's final papers and makes us recognize in him one of the great poets of the human soul. But the scientist in him could not rest until he had also calculated through intellect a way to rescue us from our desperate state.

"If there is a God," Pascal reasoned, "He is infinitely incomprehensible, since, having neither parts nor limits, He has no relation to us. We are then incapable of knowing either what He is, or if He is." If God exists, He is a "Hidden God" and unknowable to us.

It is nature's silence about the existence of God that creates the uncertainty that makes us human. We desire a home in this world and the next. That is what we know about ourselves. But we do not know—and can never know—whether we have one in either.

Confronting this mystery, Pascal thought that life could be analyzed like a game in which players roll the dice in ignorance of the outcome. He had already made a name for himself throughout Europe by devising mathematical formulas to calculate the odds that governed these entertainments. Now he proposed a mathematical solution to the game of life.

The players in this gamble must calculate the risks of believing that there is a God and that He will provide us with what we so pitifully desire. They must weigh these risks against the chance that there is no God and that we are alone. Then they must make their choice.

Pascal summed up his solution to this dilemma in the famous fragment 233: "A game is being played at the extremity of this infinite distance where heads or tails will turn up. God is, or He is not.... What will you wager? Weigh the gain and the loss in wagering that God is.... If you gain, you gain all; if you lose, you lose nothing. Wager, then, without hesitation that He is."

This solution to life's riddle is known as "Pascal's Wager," and its bottom line is this: Since you cannot know, it is better for you to believe than not.

This advice obviously makes sense, but can it make an unbeliever *believe*? Can a mathematical argument inspire a religious faith? Pascal knew it could not. In an even more famous fragment (277), he wrote, "The heart has its reasons, which reason does not know." His scientific head may have been skeptical, but Pascal was not. "Faith," he said, "is God felt by the heart."

As my own death approaches, I weigh the life I have lived against what it might have been. I ask myself: Could I have been wiser? Could I have done more? When I look at my life this way from the end, I can take satisfaction that I mostly gave it my all and did what I could. Perhaps I might have achieved greater heights; certainly I could have spent fewer days in pain. But I have no cause to think that, given who I was, my life could have turned out much better. Considering the bad choices I sometimes made, it could have been a lot worse.

It is the certainty of death that finally makes a life acceptable. When we live as fully as we can, what room is left for regret? The poet Eliot observed that there are no lost causes because there are no won causes. Everything falls to the same imperfection. One day, without exception, we will follow the same arc to earth.

These are the thoughts of resignation and acceptance that pass through my head. But in my heart are
memories of my mother and father, the home I once
had in theirs, the knowledge that they have gone before
me and that soon I will join them. Saul Bellow's mother
is there and Christopher's too. I do not have the faith
of Pascal, but I know its feeling. While reason tells me
the pictures will stop, I will be unafraid when death
comes. I will feel my way toward the horizon in front
of me, and my heart will take me home.

Blaise Pascal was born in 1623 in the region of Cler-
mont-Ferrand in France. In an open field in this place
more than five hundred years earlier, Pope Urban II
had launched the First Crusade to the Holy Land. Here,
Pascal's mother, a pious woman named Antoinette,
gave birth to three children and died when her last,
Blaise, was only three years old.

After his mother's death, Pascal's family moved to
Paris and his father, a learned man, took up the
education of his prodigy son. By the time he was twelve
years old, Pascal had proved Euclid's 32nd theorem by
himself. By the time he was twenty-eight, he had completed most of the scientific work for which he is
remembered. In the same year, his father died and his

beloved sister Jacqueline renounced the world and with-drew to a convent.

Three years after his father's death, Pascal had a religious vision, which is as famous as his scientific laws. He called it his "night of fire." Between eleven and midnight Pascal encountered, in his words, "the God of Abraham, Isaac and Jacob and not of the philosophers." No one knows exactly what he meant by this, but it has been assumed ever since that he was referring to the actual presence of God and not just the idea of Him. After this experience, Pascal became even more remote, and wrote of his "extreme aversion for the beguilements of the world." Unlike his sister, he did not completely retreat from the company of others, but began to focus his genius more and more on religious questions and, in particular, the problem of last things.

Pascal's body was as weak as his mind was strong. Since infancy, he had been afflicted by poor health and as an adult experienced stomach disorders and migraines that blurred his vision and made it difficult for him to work. By the time he reached his thirty-fifth year, he was in such pain that he had to suspend his intellectual effort. In the midst of this agony, he wrote another literary fragment, which he titled *A Prayer to Ask God to Make Good Use of Sickness*, and returned to work.

To distract himself from his physical pain, Pascal took up the problem of the cycloid, and wrote a hundred-page paper that made significant contributions to the theory of integral calculus. But his main effort was a book of religious philosophy in which he intended to justify the Christian faith. While pain made him so pitiable that his sister Gilberte wondered if his existence could be truly called a life, he went about jotting down his thoughts on scraps of paper, cutting them with scissors and binding them with thread.

As the days of his sickness gathered, neither his failing condition nor his spiritual intensity showed any signs of abating, while his life became steadily more stoic and austere. He gave away his possessions to the poor, and gradually withdrew from the friends who loved him. "It is unjust that men should attach themselves to me," he wrote in fragment number 471, "even though they do it with pleasure and voluntarily. I should deceive those in whom I had created this desire. For I am not the end of any, and I have not the wherewithal to satisfy them. Am I not about to die?"

He was. In June 1662, Pascal took in a family that was homeless. Soon after their arrival, they developed symptoms that revealed they had smallpox. But rather than put them back on the street, Pascal left his own house and moved in with his brother-in-law. Shortly after the move, he was seized with a violent illness, and on August 19 he died. He was thirty-nine years old.

The last words that Blaise Pascal uttered were these: "May God never abandon me." They reflect how helpless, uncertain and alone this passionate and brilliant and famous man felt as he passed to his own horizon.

I understand Pascal's judgment that since we are born to die it is an injustice that others should love us. But what did he propose to do with their affections? When I had more years than Pascal, I fell in love with a woman who was much younger. Our age difference was a matter of concern to me, but not from Pascal's perspective—the view from the end. Undoubtedly I should also have had generous thoughts, like him, about the effect my leaving might have on her life, since I was bound to make her a widow. But selfishly I didn't and— since she also loved me—what could I have done if I had such thoughts? In my passion, I didn't even think about the end, but drew strength from her youth and saw only the life in front of me. That was my turntable.

Pascal is right that death is many injustices in one. But what can we do about this fact except learn to live with our fate, and make use of what we have learned?

TWO

Life Is a Hospital

I WAS SIXTY-TWO YEARS OLD WHEN I BEGAN these reflections in the spring of 2001, a time fixed in my mind by the events that followed. It was a period when my work required me to travel frequently. In the solitude of planes, high above the clouds, I began to think about the summary lessons of my life, and how I might structure a text in which to set them down. It was undoubtedly the setting that inspired the project. Although air travel has been around long enough to be normal, it still feels like an unnatural exercise of human powers and makes us think of death every time we climb aloft. I jotted the first notes of this book on a yellow pad in an airport lounge, waiting for the flight to take me home.

The idea was this: If you stick around long enough to become familiar with the routines, you get a chance to see around the edges of what's going on. The passage of time allows you to weigh what people say against what they do, to see through the poses they strike and the alibis they make, and to discover how the inattention of others makes all this deviousness work. This is no small matter, because if you look long and hard enough you will find that a lie is at the root of most human wrong.

If you last long enough and get to look over collective shoulders and measure the consequences, eventually you achieve life's most irreversible result, which is the loss of innocence, the illusion that anything can happen and the hope that it will. This is a particularly destructive error. For if anything is possible, then nothing is necessary, and no conclusion follows. Consequently, no consideration can become a caution and no principle a restraint. The desire for more than is possible is the cause of greater human misery than any other.

Therefore recognition of consequences is the beginning of wisdom. In *Ravelstein,* Bellow summarizes in a single image the importance of death in making us wise: "Death is the dark backing a mirror needs if we are to see anything," he wrote. The idea I had in the airport was to view it all from the vantage of the end.

The eighteenth-century lexicographer Samuel Johnson is remembered, in part, for a famous observation he made about executions. "When a man knows he is to be hanged in a fortnight," Dr. Johnson observed, "it concentrates his mind wonderfully." It is the timeline that sets the mark and focuses the attention. Who doesn't know that death is waiting? But who plans their day with the end in mind? Eventually you may get far enough along that it is a prudence to greet each morning as though it were your last. But until then, the end is only a distant horizon silently nearing. It approaches so slowly that you can hardly see it move. Then, a day comes, perhaps when you have already reached middle age, that its shadow enters the corner of your eye and remains there, and for a dreadful beat shuts everything down.

To measure the time I had left, I began to develop the habit of looking back over twenty-year patches to see how much living had been packed into the interval. When I turned forty, this retrospect fixed me as a young man just out of college and newly married. It was 1959 and I had loaded my first car, a used Volkswagen "bug," with books and clothes and household belongings, and set out for California. Sitting beside me was my bride, who would bear me four children in the course of the next decade, and before us a horizon of uncharted distances and adventures unknown.

Twenty years does not seem a long time from some perspectives, but from others it can seem like an ample quotient. I was only forty, but the road I had traveled since setting out on this journey included a life derailed by tragedy, a marriage failed, a family grown and a career undone. It was enough to approximate an existence in full. The young groom in the picture was as strange to me now as the toddler twenty years before would have seemed to him. If my first two intervals had encompassed so much, I reasoned, there was still a lifetime ahead before I reached sixty. So why think about the end at all?

I remember the precise moment I started this clock in a London townhouse, in the autumn of 1964. I had become restless in California, where we set up our first household, and wanted more of the world than I had seen until then. In 1962 I moved our little family of three to Europe and eventually to England, where we settled in a basement flat near Hampstead Heath, on a street lined with sycamores like the neighborhood in Sunnyside.

One afternoon when the leaves had already fallen, we were enjoying a social chat in the living room of another American couple who lived on the block. The husband was not ten years older than I, but already suffused with a sadness that hinted at battles irretrievably lost. His name was Goodheart, and later he became a minor literary critic and the author of a book called *Desire and Its Discontents,* a title that seemed apt for his disposition. In the middle of the conversation, and without connecting his comment to any of its threads, he said, "We're all going to die." Then as if to retrieve the moment, he added, "I guess I've spoiled the party," which he certainly had.

I only saw Goodheart once again after that. It was more than thirty years later at an academic conference in Boston, where we sat down in a cafeteria to reminisce about the past. He had aged much as I expected he would, with his shoulders slightly stooped and the same vague despondency shadowing his eyes. I noticed that all the time we talked, a smile never crossed his lips. The tracks of age—wrinkled brow and wisps of hair whitening at the temples—had only deepened the impression of defeat.

For many years, the timekeeping I began in the Goodhearts' living room nearly provided the reassurance I craved. It allowed me to recover innocence, time without an endpoint. But the deception remained imperfect. Though I was comfortable on my turntable, I could never again completely free myself from the knowledge that I was not standing still. The effort was not helped by the signs that had begun to mark my own temporal vessel. Small physical irritations that kept me awake—an unfamiliar ache, stiffness in the joints, elusive light the eyes could no longer absorb—all served to remind me of the horizon ahead.

Yet it was not all slippage. The longer I lasted, the more flexible some faculties became. There was a cunning in age that kept the interest awake. Even as light failed, the interior eye gained depth of perception. All arcs, it turned out, are not equal, and some sinews are strengthened by what they endure. In my case, the arduous labors of the written word had gradually transformed themselves into a kind of pleasure. The mastery through artifice of worldly incoherence began to provide comforts that approached a religious consolation.

Among the discoveries of time, on the other hand, was the revelation that the spirit ages too. It gets used to what it has seen, and it sees the wall coming. Even this prospect doesn't slow us down all at once. As creatures we are endlessly devious and resourceful, prodigies in the art of self-delusion. To beat the odds, we hoodwink ourselves into idylls of recaptured youth, dallying with the young and indulging their daydreams. But inevitably a point comes when all devices fail, and we wake to the fact that the past is irretrievable and there is no way back.

In my fifth decade, I observed my children having children of their own. The new families were entirely familiar, the miracle of immanence in the flesh and the fierce bond of filial connection. Yet nothing was the same. The mark of parenthood was the responsibility for a life. But this responsibility was no longer mine. My children were accountable for their own lives now, and for my grandchildren's as well. It was a microcosm of how the world itself was passing me by. All around, others were stepping up. Swifter souls on the make, quicker minds addressing the tasks I once set for myself. It would all go on without me.

In my new household, a similar sea change had taken place. A second family was, to be sure, a kind of beginning again. There was the seductive, risk-scented encounter with a stranger, new intimacy discovered and the comforts it brought. There were the expectations that flow from unknown futures, and the energies such hopes inspire. But "beginning again" is an oxymoron. You can't really go back to where you have been before and pretend it is entirely new. This time you can see around the corners of the story you are creating and get a good idea where it will end.

While I pushed forward in denial as though time didn't matter, my younger wife took note of my progress and calculated the odds. As love deepened and entangled us, our shared joys became a cause of concern. She began to worry about a future without me, and how she might fare when I was gone. In the anxious moments these thoughts created, she made me promise to live to the age of Methuselah, to which I happily agreed. But she also insisted on knowing the practical arrangements I might make for her in the event of my death. Even this pragmatism, I noted, was a form of denial. What security could I give her for her life after ours? Was not Pascal right about this too? The love of someone will change you forever.

We had recently moved into the eyrie on the palisades with a mortgage significantly higher than that of our previous residence. To make the purchase I had undertaken a risk so large that at times it seemed I had a fingernail grip on the cliff itself. It was my wife, still full of the future, who had been looking for a new place and located the house. My calculations showed that buying the property would be imprudent. We might make the down payment and meet the mortgage for perhaps a year, but to live in the house longer would require me to double my income. As we drove to the site I braced myself to resist her desire, repeating silently the mantra I had designed. "It's not the time for us to buy; we can't afford this; the answer is no." But the instant I crossed the threshold and saw the face of the ocean pressing through a wall of windows in our new living room, I blurted *yes*.

I thought: *I am sixty-one years old, and this is my only life. If I do not seize the opportunity and attempt to make it work, I will die without ever having another chance to live this way. I am not going to miss it.* I did not want to hear the buzzer ring without taking the shot.

We bought the house and it immediately became a spur to late ambitions, the skeleton of a life on which

I would be forced to put new flesh. I took on another career, seeking rewards for my efforts that I would not have asked before. I explored different dimensions of my craft. I had been given a new way to think about what lay ahead.

The mortgage for the eyrie was nearly twice that of the house we sold. As a result, the life insurance I had taken out to pay off the old place in the event of my death was about half what the new one would require. For the first year I pushed this deficit to the back of my mind. But in the second, when my insurance agent asked if I wanted to extend the coverage, I told him to submit a proposal. Even as I did, it occurred to me that the phrase "life insurance" was itself a monument to human futility, one more gesture of impotence in our lost battles against time. Nonetheless, the policy would be immediately useful in calming April's unease.

A week after I signed the documents, a casually dressed and slightly overweight woman appeared at our door. She was a peripatetic physician who represented a company called Porta-Doctor, a name that fitted form to function. She came carrying her laboratory with her—a small white scale, a laptop to run electrocardiograms, blood pressure apparatus and a cluster of disposable syringes. With my father's ocean as our backdrop, the Porta-Doctor administered the tests required by the actuaries to establish that I had enough time ahead of me to make a good return on the insurance company's investment.

I was reasonably certain that I would be around for a while, because four months earlier I had passed my annual checkup with decent marks. Although the test numbers were as obscure to me as the Eleusian mysteries, I took the good news on my doctor's word. The annual ritual had become a lesson in the arcane religion of modern science. There were good lipids and bad, and cholesterol levels that one should not exceed. I learned about "prostate specific antigens" or "PSAs," which were the telltale indicators of a prostate disorder, a condition so common in men that it was almost a sign of age. When my tests came back, my PSA was 4.2, only marginally higher than the bar that was considered normal and no different from the year before. It was only half the levels of my two closest friends, Peter Collier and Wally Nunn.

Wally had been a helicopter gunner in Vietnam and was a stoic optimist. He didn't expect more out of life than he was likely to get, and had made it through three biopsies on his prostate gland. This was a discomfiting process that was akin to having a gun barrel shoved up your colon and needles shot into its interior walls. Each time Wally went in for the procedure, his view was that he probably didn't have a malignancy, but if he did, he would deal with it. It would be no different from surviving the war. It was still the territory, only this time of age.

Peter followed an opposite approach, expecting bad news with every outcome. His mind ran quickly to the negative and often to its extreme. Each time he went to see the urologist, he was sure he had cancer. It was his form of insurance. He would feel his way into the danger and prepare for the worst. The strategy was based in family reality. He had lost his father to the disease and his mother was dead from it as well. Long before Peter's levels rose, he had concluded that he was destined to follow them. But he didn't. His was the reverse of Pascal's Wager. Low expectations allowed him to be happily surprised every time he was wrong and survived.

The architecture of human character sorts us into pessimists like Peter and optimists like Wally and me. We don't choose these dispositions so much as they choose us. The interesting question is this: If the choice were yours, which would it be? Would you rather expect the good and be surprised when it didn't happen, or be ready for the bad and surprised when it did? Studies show that optimists actually have a better time of it and lead more successful lives. This is a predictable result since optimists focus on opportunities and the future, while pessimists dwell on problems and the past.

Yet the studies don't account for individual differences or the occasions when optimism takes a cockeyed turn and sets you up for a fall.

According to the medical numerology, I was a little overweight and my cholesterol level was on the borderline of concern. But the electrocardiogram revealed a heart in good shape. This was a reassuring sign since the cells of the heart follow my father's prescription and do not regenerate but wear steadily down to the end.

The only glitch was a urinary infection my doctor couldn't explain. The antibiotic he prescribed cleared it up, but he referred me to a urologist for a routine check just to be safe. When the test results came in negative, the doctor gave me a pass. I might not make it to Methuselah's age, but I had a good shot at getting as far as my parents, which still seemed a long way off.

When weeks had passed since the Porta-Doctor's visit and the insurance company had still not notified me that the policy was in effect, I called the agent about the delay. Apologetically, he told me that the tests had shown a spike in my PSA level. It was now 6.0, exceeding the bar that the company had set to exclude risky cases. They had rejected my application. Instead of being concerned by the news, however, the optimist in me was irritated, even indignant. I explained to the agent that his results could not be accurate because a specialist, and not just a Porta-Doctor with her office in a bag, had recently given me a clean bill of health. I needed the insurance and demanded another test.

The Porta-Doctor returned and we repeated the routine. This time my PSA was 5.8. The decline appeared reassuring, although I had no real under-standing of the test or what the numbers meant. When I called my doctor for his opinion, he was not so san-guine. The 30 percent increase over a four-month stretch, even from a relatively low level, set off an alarm and he sent me back to the urologist for another round. The urologist ordered a biopsy and reserved a place for me in an outpatient facility.

I had begun these tests in June and now it was the end of summer. Through all of this, I still barely knew where my prostate was located or what its function was. I have no particular excuse for this ignorance or the lack of concern that lay behind it. As with our approach to the future, each of us deals with these mat-ters differently. It is one of the habits of our being that we don't really think about, but that determine who we are. Some of us make our bodies the focus of lav-ish interest; others concentrate on feeding the soul and ignore the flesh as an unworthy vessel. Why are we so different in matters that are so fundamental? Why is it so difficult for us to change our attitudes even when we recognize how they affect our fate?

Inertias like these are the gravities that define us, their subterranean pulls more powerful than reason. (How can utopians dream of changing the world when it is so difficult to lose an inch from one's waistline?) Yet who really knows where such attitudes come from or why they persist? Why some of us are driven and others are not? Why one person devours emptiness and another is full? Why some are drawn to sorrow, while others can't wait to get up and dance?

I was a person who expended little energy in speculating on distant outcomes and who lacked a morbid interest in others' misfortunes. I had learned to live with disappointment, but expected good things to be put on my table, however implausibly. A prostate cancer was as remote from the possibilities I imagined for myself as a voyage to the moon. This complacency was not entirely unreasonable. I had inherited my mother's genes, and could not remember a day she was ill until her first stroke at eighty. Consequently, when I imagined my own future, I was always in her good health. But my mistake over the Porta-Doctor's test results had torn away the outer skin of confidence that had cocooned me since birth, and I could not suppress the feeling that I was about to be blindsided by unanticipated events.

The biopsy was conducted on September 9, 2001. Five days later, April and I headed for the urologist's office to get the doctor's report. The wait had been wearing on April, who was already testing what it might mean to share the remaining days of a terminal case, but I was glad the uncertainty would be over.

When we arrived, we discovered that the building had been evacuated earlier in the day as a result of a bomb threat. Even now it was almost deserted. My urologist had not yet finished an operation that had been delayed for hours because of the scare, and the office nurse told us he would not be available for appointments. Three days earlier, Islamic radicals had rammed commercial jetliners into the World Trade Center and the Pentagon, acts of terror that set emotions aflame. Three thousand people had been killed in the attacks, including our friend Barbara Olson. Millions of ordinary lives had been disrupted. Why should ours be unaffected? We rescheduled our visit and drove home.

In the days that followed, I watched the news and carried on my routines. Attempting to assemble a map of what might lie ahead, I took time to read some medical literature about the contagion that might be spreading inside me. A *New Yorker* article provided me with a retrospect on the "war on cancer" that the government and the medical profession had launched fifty years before. I was still in my adolescence when the first campaigns of the war had begun, as I remembered, with great fanfare and an abundance of hope. Massive public resources had been channeled into the crusade, and in the intervening years, scientists had doubled the sum of human knowledge on the subject more than once. Yet for all the effort and intelligence expended, the causes of the disease were still not understood and no cure had been found. Apparently there were limits to what the human mind could accomplish in the span of a lifetime, or at all. There was a positive side, however, in that many new treatments had been developed that were effective when the cancer was identified early.

One of the books I read was *How We Die,* by a physician named Sherwin Nuland. He described how in a cancer the cells rebel against nature's cycle, as though refusing to grow up. Like marauding slackers, they embark on an orgy of creation and destruction, multiplying without restraint and devouring everything in sight. The cancer's first cells, Nuland writes, are "the bastard offspring of unsuspecting parents who ultimately reject them because they are ugly, deformed, and unruly. In the community of living tissues, the uncontrolled mob of misfits that is cancer behaves like a gang of perpetually wilding adolescents. They are the juvenile delinquents of cellular society."

From reading *How We Die,* I discovered that my
father was not quite on the mark. The cells do not simply age and decay, but are born over and over again. It
is true that they are continually dying, but they are "constantly being replenished as they die, not only by the
reproduction of their younger survivors, but also by an
actively reproducing group of progenitors." As normal
cells mature, they assume their appointed functions in
the body and lose their ability to procreate. Whether
their job is to secrete hormones or absorb nutrients, the
more fully they perform their function, the less they
reproduce. But when cells fail to mature fully, they retain
some of their reproductive power and a cellular mass or
tumor is formed. If the process goes awry early and dramatically enough, the reproductive energy is almost infinite and the tumor will be a cancer.

These cancers behave like revolutionaries in society. Instead of serving the body and performing the
functions that keep the organism alive, the problem
cells in a narcissistic fury concentrate on the uncontrolled reproduction of themselves, feeding on the
healthy cells around them. As Dr. Nuland colorfully
describes this process, they embark on "a continuous,
uninhibited, circumferential, barn-burning expedition
of destructiveness," strangling and devouring everything in their path. Nothing escapes them, and nothing

can stop them. Defying nature's order, they do not age or even have "the decency to die when they should." The orgy of creation continues until the cancer kills the host body, and itself in the process.

Having failed to refute my blood tests, I had come to respect them. When April and I returned to the urologist's office on September 19 and I was told that I had prostate cancer, the news did not surprise or alarm me. I had anticipated the diagnosis and was prepared. When I thought about it, this was really part of the long process of dying that was my life, and indeed all our lives. It had already become familiar. Since that autumn day in the Goodhearts' living room, I had never been unaware of the steadily shrinking view in front of me.

Perhaps the fact that I had cancer should have caused me a bigger lurch than it did. But I had come to a point in my life, as I have noted, where I felt I had done pretty much what was in me to do, and had come to know what to expect. I could find satisfaction in that. I could even take pleasure in my acceptance. After the first fear, there is no other. Consequently, at the most vulnerable point of my life, I actually felt quite strong.

But April, who was sitting beside me as the doctor recounted my fate, had the wind taken out of her. When I turned in her direction, her eyes had a stricken look and her voice was stumbling over questions, giving the impression she was ducking the answers even before they came back. She was clearly off balance and my heart reached out to her, though there was nothing I could do to relieve her suffering.

In the time I had known her, I had grown to love this woman of my twilight years with an abandon I would not previously have thought possible. I had logged so much time in what seemed now like other lives that a renewal of faith appeared unlikely. But there we were, deep in, and I was sorry to see her enduring such pain.

Shuffling the medical reports on his desk, the urologist unveiled a new aspect of the numerology, explaining that the biopsy slides revealed a "Gleason 6," which was a formula for quantifying the density and mass of the cancer and calculating its rate of growth. My ranking turned out to be not so bad. It indicated that the tumor was contained in the prostate sac and could be removed by surgery. In other cases, where the cancer escaped into the bones or the lymph system, the odds grew longer.

The doctor checked off these details along with my medical options in a formulaic drone that was irritating. When I tried to ask a question, he brushed it aside with schoolmaster severity. I would have to wait, he admonished, until he completed his list. His formality was a full-disclosure mode, the product of the malpractice torts that had become a kind of exoskeleton of the medical profession. I listened as my treatment options were put on the table. Radiation might remove the cancer or it might not. But if it did not work, the treatments would damage the tissues so severely as to make an operation impossible. There were hormone therapies available too.

My attention wandered as he described these choices. Altering hormones seemed to be playing with the very structures of feeling and being, and, like radiation, didn't have the certainty of a cure. Besides, April had already decided that if the diagnosis was cancer we were going to cut. "We're not going to take a chance with your life," she said. "I can't lose you." I was sufficiently touched by her concern that I hardly noticed she was making a crucial decision for me. Her passion made it feel like the choice was mine.

The drone continued. The operation was called a "radical prostatectomy." It would require four and a half hours and would involve "a lot of blood." He would schedule the operation for the following month. He wanted me to come into the office each of the three weeks prior to the date to donate blood "in case we need it." Impotence was an expected result for "about half" the patients. (The incontinence rate was lower and I thoughtlessly discounted it.) Even with all the bloodletting and the downside possibilities, he cautioned, there was still no guarantee that the cancer would be entirely removed. "But if we don't get it this way, we can follow up with radiation afterwards, and hope that works."

As we were driving home, April turned to me, her eyes red with worry, and said, "I never thought you would get sick. I thought if you were not going to die of old age, you would die in a car accident or someone would shoot you." Dramatic as these fears sounded, they had a basis. I was a controversial public figure, sometimes inspiring passionate threats. Even if I wasn't going to be the target of a deranged opponent, I was at risk on other counts. I was a distracted pedestrian and driver, often drifting mentally and forgetting where I was. It was not a lack of focus so much as a focus misplaced. My thoughts sometimes caused me to be drawn so far into interior space that the environment outside faded to black.

"I never thought you would get cancer," she continued her regrets. "You were always so healthy." As she said this, I detected in her tone a false hope that the diagnosis would prove mistaken. I, myself, never doubted that it was correct. Perhaps because I had been so healthy throughout my life and had seen so many others suffer, it occurred to me that it would only be fair if my time had come. As if this were a consideration in nature's court.

Even after we left the doctor's office, I was unable to think of myself as a victim. My father had warned me that life was terminal and mine had not been so bad; from where he stood, it had been better than I had a right to expect. "You lead a charmed life," he said once, provoking me at the time. But the observation had earned a grudging respect ever since, for indeed I had. If not nine lives, I had been granted more than one man's share. Besides, I had already felt the chill of my mortality, and seen the wall coming. I was not a young man and I had lived longer than Pascal.

After leaving the urologist's office, April and I compared notes and agreed to seek another opinion. This course had been urged on me by my friend Peter, who seemed at times more worried about my health than I was. He wanted me to consult a doctor with a residency in a teaching hospital to be sure of benefiting from the latest knowledge and the most skilled surgical hands.

But while Peter and April were already deep into worst-case scenarios, I stubbornly was not. The cancer had been discovered in time and I was mostly confident that it would be cured. On the other hand, my

PSA level had risen rapidly between the tests and had fooled me once. One might see the calm I was experiencing as fortitude, but also as delusion. Since there was not much I could do to affect the outcome, it didn't really matter which.

My friend Wally suggested that I read Patrick Walsh's *Guide to Surviving Prostate Cancer*. A surgeon at Johns Hopkins, Walsh was famous for the percentage of his patients who emerged from surgery with their sexual and bladder functions intact. From Walsh's book I learned that a majority of men have a prostate cancer embedded in their soma, which is one of the many seeds of mortality waiting in ambush in the landscape of the flesh. I also learned that the name "prostate" derives from the Greek word for "protector," an irony since the gland seems anything but.

While the prostate's positive functions are obscure, its location creates significant problems if anything should go wrong, particularly if the remedy involves cutting. "Although it's only as big as a walnut, the prostate is a miniature Grand Central Station, a busy hub at the crossroads of a man's urinary and reproductive tracts. . . . It is tucked away deep within the pelvis, surrounded by vulnerable structures—the bladder, the rectum, the sphincters responsible for urinary control, major arteries and veins, and a host of delicate nerves, some of them so tiny that we've only

recently discovered them." In other words, if some-
body is planning to prune this area with a knife, he'd
better have a clear idea of what is to be cut and where
it is, along with the dexterity to do only that.

Walsh advised patients to look for a surgeon with
"nerves of steel." The reason was that a radical prostatectomy was "one of the most difficult" surgeries in
medicine and could include "tremendous, sometimes
life-threatening blood loss." This was hardly reassuring. The professional grit was necessary to prevent a
surgical panic in the event the incision produced a "sea
of blood" obscuring the tissues to be cut. Among those
that should not be cut were the neurovascular bundles
that produced erections. The distance separating the
targeted prostate from these bundles was a mere five
millimeters, making impotence a hair away if the scalpel
slipped. Walsh had pioneered in anatomical discoveries that reduced the blood flow dramatically. This
enabled him to perform the first prostate operation that
preserved the filaments. In April 1982, the operation
was performed on a fifty-two-year-old patient, who
recovered his potency within a year.

In other words, the most important service a patient
could provide for himself was to find a surgeon who
knew what he was doing. Walsh had concrete sugges-
tions as to how a layman could make this assessment.
The simplest and most direct was to ask how much

time the doctor estimated the operation would take. A skilled surgeon who had mastered the anatomy could perform the task in two hours. This was half the time that the Cedars-Sinai urologist was proposing to me.

As Walsh described it, a radical prostatectomy had three goals: "First is removing the cancer, then preserving urinary continence, and then preserving sexual function. In that order." To underscore the point he added: "The primary goal is not to preserve potency. It is to get rid of the cancer ...." Why did men need the underscoring? Why did we fear the loss of potency even before we feared death? When faced with the alternatives, April had not hesitated before opting for the surgical cut. "Your life is more important than sex," she said. I had reached a point in my own arc where I felt ready to accept this outcome. It was just part of the leaving, which had begun long ago.

It was not that stark a concession, moreover, since an orgasm was a nerve response in the brain. Removal of the prostate only eliminated the ability to ejaculate — not inconsequential, but not the end of the world. The tremors, the release, the elation would still be there, although never quite the same. But then nothing was quite the same. I had lost more than a few abilities already. I was sure I could handle this.

April and I made an appointment with a new surgeon named Donald Skinner, who was head of the

Urology Department at the University of Southern California and a noted figure in the field. I had come to him through the good graces of my friend Helene Galen, who was able to get me to the head of a three-month waiting list. Helene was all too familiar with hospitals. Her husband, Lou, a lovable curmudgeon, had spent nearly a year in intensive care, semi-comatose with complications of the heart, before miraculously coming through. Life was just that precarious.

During one of my visits to see Skinner, a young doctor in the building informed me that the university had built the eight-story Norris Cancer Clinic around Skinner's practice. While waiting for the examination, I asked his nurse, Steve, how I would go about giving blood for the operation. Steve said, "Oh, he never takes blood. He wants you to go in on a full tank." My confidence level, already unwarrantedly high, rose with his words.

Adding to this encouragement, Steve noted that my PSA level was low. How high could it go? I asked. "Well," he said, "Egypt's foreign minister had a PSA of 110. They flew him in from Cairo, but when he arrived here we had to send him back for hormone treatments to bring it down low enough so that he could be operated on." Steve also let me know how fortunate I was to have discovered the cancer early. Telly Savalas, the bald actor who played the television detective "Kojak," had come in with a PSA of 10, he recalled. "Dr. Skinner scheduled the biopsy, but Savalas had a Christmas special and cancelled it. Then he needed a vacation. I called him to tell him how important it was, but he never came back. Four years later he was gone. He was fifty years old." Perhaps Kojak was afraid to face a life of diminished returns.

A silver-haired gentleman now entered the room to tower over me. His smile was accented by a mild jut of the jaw and a manner that was almost jovial. Before putting on white surgical gloves, he made a sexual quip about those he had passed up in their box on the counter, which were an uncommon purple. I didn't feel trivialized by the humor so much as relieved. When he discussed the impending procedure, his tone conveyed the impression that the carving of my flesh would be no more problematic than preparing a roast.

"How long will he be on the operating table?" my wife asked.

"An hour and a half."

"Should he donate blood?"

"No, there won't be any need."

Like the Cedars-Sinai doctor, Skinner went over my options point by point. He had taken a look at the biopsy and concluded that it was a Gleason 7—one grade higher than I had been told. Evidently, there was more a surgeon had to get right than the angle of the

cut. The new Gleason standard suggested that there
might be leakage and that the operation would not
remove all the cancer. If this proved right, I would have
to undergo radiation, with no certainty about the outcome. On the other hand, Skinner was as confident
that I shouldn't worry about this, as he was that the
cutting would be routine.

Before we left, I mentioned the Walsh book. Aware
that I was nearly sixty-three, Skinner said knowingly,
"Walsh doesn't take patients over sixty." I picked up
the cue: "That's because Walsh wants to keep his per-
centages high."

My only regret was that I couldn't share the confidence I was now feeling with April, who was moving
quietly beside me, her eyes still wounded. Instead of
lifting her spirits, the new details had only sharpened
our reality and deepened her distress. When I glanced
in her direction, I would catch her looking off into the
distance, turning her head from me as if to hide her
thoughts.

Periodically, she would come back from these private spaces, protective as ever, to entertain me with flir-
tatious daydreams she spun out of the very darkness
of her fears. Now she was my nurse, pushing me around
in my wheelchair, conjuring the sensual pleasures of
our invalid life together on the other side of the ordeal.
Her marital solidarity was an even greater reassurance

than Skinner's expertise and made me love her all the more.

How did she love me? Could I ever really count the ways? When you have passed beyond a first marriage, the conjugal mystery inevitably deepens. You have stepped off a coastal shelf into waters where the past works relentlessly against you. Alien corners of the human personality have become familiar. You have met the mercurial elements of the human soul, and know how they can turn on you and break your heart.

Alone with these thoughts, watching my wife grieve for me while I was still alive, I felt almost grateful for my condition. April was twenty-two years younger than I, by my private calendar the equivalent of a life-time. If I were to go now, she would have a lifetime in front of her. Her lineage, which was an uncommon blend of Cherokee and Gael, had graced her with green eyes set off by high cheekbones and sensuous lips. A regal carriage lent her an aristocratic air. When we stepped out in public together I sensed how others were unable to pass without turning to take her in. I knew she could have her pick of suitors if she so cared. Instead she was fearful of a life without me. There she was attending my crippled future, spinning through her tears the tapestries of joys we would share in my con-valescence. I realized that through my illness I had been given a rare gift, the knowledge of my wife's heart.

I didn't spend any time thinking about the cut that Skinner was preparing, which I understood from Walsh's text would stretch from the navel to the groin. Nor did I try to picture myself anesthetized and splayed like a laboratory specimen on his operating table. It was the rule I followed in life generally: not to waste time worrying about what I could not control. Once the anesthesia was in the tube, I was removed from my own fate. It was left to April to soldier through it.

Coming back, my memories are fogged and disjointed. A cup of ice chips; a frenzy at the bedside as my blood pressure rose; an anxious team scrambling to bring it down; a code blue called over the public address system and somewhere down the hall a family keening when the emergency was over. But I remember clearly the warm lips of my life mate and her comforting words through the darkness, at my side, carrying me through.

On the third day, the hospital released me. April had hired a male nurse named Sam to help her through the first day of my convalescence at home. I was hooked up to a catheter and drain, and had a ten-inch oozing wound in my abdomen. The open sore had to be regularly swabbed with Betadine to protect it from infection. I was disoriented and groggy from the anesthetic and irritated with the well-meaning nurse, who had become the symbol of my helpless state.

The irritation I now displayed was one of the less admirable traits I had inherited from my father. Painfully self-conscious, he suffered greatly from the indignities that his maladies forced on him in age. He had made many trips to the hospital for hip replacements and repairs. As a patient he was ferocious, venting his frustration on the nurses who ministered to him, as though they were the instigators of his distress. I was almost no better. When Sam approached my bedside I looked away and demanded my wife, disliking myself even as I did. When April came in his stead it was a balm to my savaged soul.

Within days of her ministrations I was feeling well enough to resume work and, improbable though it was, did so. April had bought me a bed desk, which straddled my legs and allowed me to use a laptop from my prone position so I could continue the text I had been writing. Although my mind was still webby from the anesthetic and my body inert, I was in unusually good spirits and resumed my narrative. Perhaps it was just a way of averting my attention from present trials, but I was feeling revived and free.

After a week of convalescence I was up and about, and then out as well. Diapered and dragging my catheter and bag concealed under my suit, I appeared on a national radio show, to the consternation of its host, and gave a speech at a formal dinner, though by the end of the three-hour evening I was so drained that April suggested the guests were probably counting the days I had left. On her advice, I deferred further appearances until I was in better shape and could do them without the medical appliances.

Three weeks after the operation, I returned to the hospital for their removal. The first device to be extracted was the one technically known as an "indwelling Foley catheter." The almost spiritual name identified a tube rudely inserted through the urinary tract into the bladder. At the inner end of the tube was a balloon, inflated with liquid to keep the whole apparatus from slipping out. It had been inserted while I was under the anesthetic. I was not so lucky for the extraction, which proved to be physically discomfiting although not the most brutal part of the process. As I stood at attention for the catheter maneuver, Skinner cradled my organ in a sanitary napkin, turned to April and said, "Did you bring the mustard?" "Mustard?" she asked as he yanked, and it was out.

After that came the drainage tube, whose withdrawal was as painful a procedure as I had experienced. When the device was pulled from my abdomen, I was left sweating and shaking. Still a bit wobbly after putting on my clothes, I bumped into the doorframe trying to exit the room. "Are you all right?" my wife voiced a serious concern. "I'm just trying to make Skinner laugh," I said.

With the catheter gone, I was ready to gauge how skillful his knife had been. In my readings in the literature, I had come across cases of postoperative men whose incontinence caused them to go through eighteen diapers a day, a nightmare to contemplate. Fortunately, Skinner had not failed me. Within a few days I was able to get by with two or three, and within a week had resumed my work schedule and was traveling across the country making speeches to large audiences. By the end of one speech I was so tired that halfway through the question period I didn't have the energy to vocalize my thought, even after I had managed to get it from the top of my brain to the tip of my tongue.

The operation caused me to reflect on the way vital aspects of our being hang by slender corporal threads. A nerve bundle millimeters in diameter, a slice of tissue almost invisible to the human eye could change you forever. As it was, my sexual function also returned, so I could consider myself, in a manner of speaking, restored. Months after the first post-op check, I wrote a note of thanks to Skinner. I began by observing that his bedside manner had so disarmed me during my previous visit that it made the occasion seem perfectly routine. As a result, I had failed to adequately express my gratitude:

"I have read enough now to know that my return to almost normal life is as close to a miracle as most of us are likely to get. Before the operation I had set my mind to accept what might come, which I expected would probably include radical changes in my life. Now as I realize how familiar my body feels and how intact my life is, I wonder how I would be feeling if you and your skills had not made that possible. Would I have been able to be as stoic and as strong as I had hoped? I am grateful that I don't have to know the answer to that question."

It hardly seemed sufficient. What could words express in matters like this? When I mentioned my good fortune to another surgeon at the cancer center, she said, "Dr. Skinner is as close as you can get to the hands of God."

I was not out of the woods. When Skinner examined the gland he had removed, he noted a stickiness in the walls indicating that the cancer could have leaked from the prostate sac into the bones or possibly the lymph. He ordered treatments and sent me to see his colleague, a radiologist named Oscar Streeter, a likeable man even larger physically than Skinner, and as dark of complexion as Skinner was light. April, who had a talent for photography, visualized a dramatic shot of the two of them towering over me in their white smocks with my diminutive self framed between.

The contrast went below the surface. Where Skinner was understated and reserved, Streeter was voluble and engaging. Both, however, were aggressively good-natured. Conversing with them, you could almost forget you were in a cancer ward surrounded by cruelties that not even their skills could meliorate. Perhaps that was the point. Perhaps their good humor was also a shield they had developed against the occasions when their imperfect science was bound to fail.

Streeter scheduled a series of treatments over the next three months. Every weekday morning, April and I would get into her blue Pathfinder and she would drive us along the Santa Monica freeway to the radiation center at Norris. En route, I would force down a quart of water as Streeter had instructed. The objective was to fill the bladder so that it would push aside some of my internal parts and provide a better target for the x-rays. Once we arrived, April would wait in the parking lot outside, feeding carrot sticks to our caramel Shih-Tzu astride her lap, while I sat in the waiting room studying the faces of my new community until I was called in for the five-minute session.

In the center of the treatment room was a table engulfed by an x-ray machine, whose giant arm rotated a beam vertically around the patient. A bank of computers guided the beam to the site in my groin area, whose latitudes a technician had marked with tattoo points. The ceiling of the room had been painted with clouds as in a child's nursery, a graphic fantasy of heaven that lent a surreal effect. Recessed speakers piped in popular tunes, and an irritating buzzer went off when the beam was activated. I felt nothing, but then I had not felt the cancer either.

I could not say the same for the after-effects. Coming out into the southern California sun, I was overcome by a wooziness that lasted most of the day. The nausea reminded me of the anesthetic gas I had been given at the dentist's office when I was a youngster, before the discovery of Novocaine. I had recurring images of my childhood dentist Reggie, dead now thirty or forty years, but like my new doctors an inveterate kidder.

As we drove back through the haze of late morning traffic, life was going on in its normal rush. Lines of commuters were headed toward their appointments in a way that I no longer was. Like my fellow patients, I had entered a state of suspended animation, and was bound by the knowledge that my freedom was not forever and not an escape.

Day in and day out, my wife prayed for my health and for my continued presence on this earth. Her brother Joe and his wife, Martha, who attended a

Catholic church, St. John Vianney, had organized thirty Hispanic men, women and children, including my nieces, to pray for me too. Every morning these relatives and strangers whispered my name in their intimate conversations with God, and implored Him to spare me. Others did too. I was touched and strengthened by their love and by their answered prayers. I was saved—at least for the moment—and was grateful for that. I would be able to share life with April again, to be with my children and grandchildren, to rise in the morning and greet the sea.

Was God really behind this good fortune? Had He intervened to save an agnostic soul as a reward to the believers? Thankful as I was for their concern, I didn't like to think so. For if He had saved me to answer their prayers, then I would also have to hold Him responsible for the others whose prayers had not been answered.

One of the patients who came regularly at my appointed time was a young woman who seemed to be in her twenties. She did not come in from the parking lot where her husband might be waiting for her as my wife did for me. She came in a wheelchair accompanied by a sad woman who appeared to be her mother and who had wheeled her to the radiation clinic from one of the recesses of the vast hospital complex we were in. She had barely begun life, but her eyes had already traveled to a distant space, displaying a vacancy that could have been equally the result of medications or resignation. For her this life had become a waiting room from which there was no exit. I could not help thinking, each time I saw her, of the many lives I had been privileged to live in my span, and those she would not.

I was acutely conscious of the inhabitants of the cancer ward whose prospects were worse than mine. Along with those who loved them they had endured multiple operations, multiple setbacks, years of a crippled existence, and a fate on hold. "Life is a hospital," the poet Eliot wrote. I could appreciate the metaphorical truth in the image, but it still felt like a violence to the reality that confronted me. Not all life's hospitals were equal and not all God's children were saved.

All my life, wherever I have been, in whatever places I have found myself, I have felt like an outsider. And who hasn't? Every home is temporary and we are only transients. But I was not prepared for the irony I encountered now, that even as a patient in a cancer ward I would feel myself an outsider. I looked at the women in their kerchiefs and wigs, and the men in the watch caps they donned to hide their baldness; I took in their gray pallor and the dark looks of the family members who came to support them, and felt, "I am not one of them."

It was the false consciousness that had accompanied me my entire life. These tragedies happen to others. I am not one of them. Even as I entertained these thoughts, I recognized how self-denying and ultimately absurd they were. None of us are outsiders. We are all going to the same destination. Though my recent ordeal was over and I could walk back into the sunlight and resume my interrupted life, I was not really out of there. I had been lucky, but I had not been given a pardon, only a reprieve. My father was right. Life is a cancer ward, and death is in our cells metastasizing every day.

THREE

On Earth As It Is in Heaven

LOVE DEATH. THIS IS THE IMPROBABLE instruction that the founder of an Egyptian sect named the Muslim Brotherhood imparted to his followers in the 1920s. A Muslim disciple named Mohammed Atta copied this instruction into his journal just before leading the attack on the World Trade Center three days before my biopsy. Was it a coincidence that this dark creed took root in a country of monuments to the quest for life beyond the grave? The sentence that Mohammed Atta actually wrote down was this: "Prepare for *jihad* and be lovers of death."

How can one love death? This is a question that is incomprehensible to us unless we are overwhelmed by personal defeats. But it is the enigma at the heart of human history, which is a narrative moved by war between men. For how can men go to war unless they love death, or a cause that is worth more than life itself?

The Muslim Brotherhood was founded in 1928, but the summons to holy war had been planted in Arab hearts more than a thousand years before. The prophet Mohammed created the Muslim faith and claimed he was fulfilling the gospel of Christ. But Mohammed was a warrior and Jesus a man of peace who instructed his followers to shun the path of history and separate the sacred from the profane. His kingdom was not of this world. *Render unto Caesar that which is Caesar's, and unto God that which is God's.* Mohammed summoned his followers to make the world a place for God, which meant conquering Caesar himself.

Sayyid Qutb, an Egyptian who was executed for treason in 1966, is recognized as the intellectual father of the Islamic *jihad*. His brother Mohammed was a teacher of its leader Osama bin Laden and his texts are read by would-be martyrs in *madrassas* across the Muslim world. The hope that consumed Sayyid Qutb's life was to establish the rule of Islam throughout the heathen nations and the Islamic *umma,* to make the world a holy place.

Sayyid Qutb regarded Christianity as a threat to this Islamic redemption. He condemned the Christians for their separation of the sacred from the profane, God's world from Caesar's. He called this division a "hideous schizophrenia," which reflected the very corruption he set out to correct. Christians had created liberal societies, Qutb said, in which "God's existence is not denied, but His domain is restricted to the heavens and His rule on earth is suspended." Islam's task was "to unite the world and the faith." It was what Jewish mystics called *tikkun olam,* a mission to repair the world by bringing about the rule of God's law on earth.

Qutb wrote this prescription in one of his most famous texts, which he titled *Social Justice in Islam.* The mission of Islam, he explained, was "to unite heaven and earth in a single system." To make the world one.

This is the totalitarian idea. When the wave of redemption is complete, nothing will remain untransformed, nothing unholy or unjust. Total transformation is the goal of all radical *jihad*s, including the flight that burned the towers of evil in Manhattan. It is the cause that Mohammed Atta served. Like all revolutionary passions, the totalitarian hope of radical Islam is to redeem the world. It is the desire to put order into our lives and to heal the wound in creation.

But there is no earthly doctor who can cure us. The practical consequence of all radical dreams, therefore, is a permanent war of faith.

Inevitably and invariably, the effort to make the world whole begins with its division into two opposing camps. In order to conduct the work of salvation, redeemers must separate the light from the darkness, the just from the unjust, the believers from the damned. For radical Muslims this division is the line separating the House of Islam from the House of War, the realm of the faithful from the world of heretics and infidels, who are impure of heart and who must be converted or destroyed.

A thousand years before Mohammed Atta left on his fatal mission, a Shi'ite named Hassan al-Sabbah began a holy war to overthrow the Muslim state. In Hassan's eyes, the Sunni caliphate that the Prophet Mohammed had established to govern Islam had already fallen into a state of corruption. It was no longer holy; it was no longer God's. To cleanse Islam and restore the faith, Hassan created a martyr vanguard, whom others referred to as the "Assassins," and whose deeds have bequeathed to us the word itself. The mission of the Assassins was to kill the apostate rulers of the false Islamic state, and purify the realm.

Because their mission was a service to God, it was considered a dishonor to return alive, and none did. The Koran assured the Assassins of the faith that the reward for the life they gave was paradise itself. "So let them fight in the way of God who sell the present life for the world to come; whosoever fights in the way of God and is slain, conquers. We shall bring him a mighty wage." When the Assassins' first victim, the vizier in Quhistan, was slain, Hassan al-Sabbah said,

"The killing of this devil is the beginning of bliss." Revolutionaries love death because it is the gate of heaven and the beginning of bliss.

Four years before 9/11, Mohammed Atta traveled to Afghanistan to join the International Islamic Front for the Holy War against Jews and Crusaders, whose leader was Osama bin Laden. Mohammed Atta was a small, wiry man, the humorless son of a demanding father. After his team of modern Assassins turned the towers in Manhattan into a smoking ruin, his father told reporters, "My son is a very sensitive man. He is soft and was extremely attached to his mother."

Before the hour of his *jihad,* on the very page where he had copied the summons to love death, Mohammed Atta acknowledged that it was a call to perform acts unnatural to men. "Everybody hates death, fears death," he wrote, but then explained why men should love it nonetheless. "Only the believers who know the life after death and the reward after death, will be the ones seeking death." Mohammed Atta had found a cause that was greater than life itself.

But was Mohammed Atta right? Did his martyrs sign up for death to gain a greater return? This presumes that the only reason people would seek to end their lives in this world is the hope of reward in another.

Do they not also run toward what they fear? When we have guilty secrets to hide, do we not find ways to end the awful wait before judgment by leaving the clues that betray us? Especially if we are withholding secrets from those we fear and love. Are we not all guilty in the eyes of God, and did not Mohammed Atta fear and love Him?

What if martyrs hate life more than they love death? If we look at the scanty record of Mohammed Atta's time on this earth, it suggests that escape was always on his mind. "Purify your heart and clean it of all earthly matters," he wrote in his instructions to his martyr team. "The time of fun and waste has gone. The time of judgment has arrived."

In his short life, Mohammed Atta does not seem to have had much room for pleasure. His father was a successful lawyer, who was ambitious and austere. The family had two residences but lived frugally and apart from others. "They didn't visit and weren't visited," said a neighbor later. The father agreed, "We are people who keep to ourselves." An adolescent friend of Mohammed's described the Atta household: "It was a house of study. No playing, no entertainment. Just study." Even as an adolescent, to avoid the contamination of the flesh Mohammed would leave the room when Egyptian television featured belly dancing programs, as it frequently did.

According to those who knew him as a young adult, Mohammed Atta was insular, religiously strict and psychologically intense. The death of an insect made him emotional; the modern world repelled him. A fellow urban planning student remembered how the usually reserved Mohammed became enraged by a hotel construction near the ancient market of Aleppo, which he viewed as the desecration of Islam's heritage. "Disneyworld," he sneered, the Crusaders' revenge. Mohammed continued to avoid sensual images, whether from television screens or wall posters. He hated and feared the female gender, averting his eyes from women who so much as neglected to cover their arms.

Others testified that he could not take pleasure in so basic and social a human act as eating. A roommate recalled that he sustained himself by spooning lumps from a heap of cold potatoes he would mash and leave on a plate in the communal refrigerator for a week at a time. A German convert who hung out with members of the terrorist cell that Atta headed thought it was his morbid seriousness that allowed him to lead others, but dismissed him derisively as a "harmless, intelligent nut." The people he lived with longed for him to leave. A girlfriend of one of them said, "A good day was when Mohammed was not home."

Five years before his appointment with death, Mohammed Atta drew up a will in which he admonished his mourners to die as good Muslims. "I don't want a pregnant woman or a person who is not clean to come and say good-bye to me because I don't approve it," he admonished. "The people who will clean my body should be good Muslims and I do not want a lot of people to wash my body unless it is necessary. The person who will wash my body near my genitals must wear gloves on his hands so he won't touch my genitals.... I don't want any women to go to my grave at all during my funeral or on any occasion thereafter."

In life, Mohammed Atta despised women, but on his way to death, he promised his martyrs many, citing the Koranic verse: "Know that the gardens of paradise are waiting for you in all their beauty and the women of paradise are waiting, calling out, 'Come hither, friend of God.' They have dressed in their most beautiful clothing."

Mohammed also wrote down these instructions for the mission ahead: "When the confrontation begins, strike like champions who do not want to go back to this world. Shout, 'Allahu Akbar [God is great],' because this strikes fear in the hearts of the nonbelievers." Whoever neglected his will or did not follow Islam, Mohammed warned, "that person will be held responsible in the end."

Like Mohammed Atta we long for the judgment that will make right what is not. We want to see virtue rewarded and the wicked rebuked. We yearn for release from the frustrations and disappointments of an imperfect life. Consequently every God of love is also a God of justice, and therefore a God of punishment and death. If this were not so, if God did not care to sort out good from evil, what would His love be worth?

The emotions of fear and hope spring from the love of self, and therefore make our motives suspect. Are those who claim to be God's warriors pure of heart and above doubt? Can men serve God if they are really serving themselves? Do martyrdoms like Mohammed Atta's represent noble aspirations, or are they merely desperate remedies for personal defeats?

Mohammed Atta was a withdrawn and ineffectual man who died without achieving his worldly ambitions. He never realized his goal of becoming an architect or an urban planner, never married or had a family. Apart from his *jihad*, Mohammed Atta never made a mark in life. But in death he was a god, bringing judgment to three thousand innocent souls.

If Allah is the maker of life, as Mohammed Atta believed, could He desire the destruction of what He had created? What is suicide but rage at the living, and contempt for the life left behind? Mohammed Atta offered his deed of destruction as a gift to God. In his eyes, his martyrdom was unselfish and the strangers he killed were not innocent. His mission was to purge the world of wasteful pleasures, to vanquish the guilty and to implement God's grace.

But if God wanted to cleanse His creation, why would He need Mohammed Atta to accomplish His will?

These are the questions of an agnostic, one who has no business saying what God desires or does not. Nonetheless, an agnostic can appreciate believers like Pascal, whose humility is transparent and who are attempting to make sense of the incomprehensible through faith. *Why are we born? Why are we here? Why do we die?* An agnostic can respect the faith of a skeptic who confronts our misery and refuses to concede defeat. He can admire a faith that provides consolation for the inconsolable, and in a heartless world finds reason to live a moral life.

But murder is not moral and the desire to redeem the world requires it. Because redemption requires the damnation of those who do not want to be saved.

My father was an atheist and embraced the secular belief of the social redeemers. Along with all who think they have practical answers to the absurd cruelties of our human lot, my father felt superior to those who do not, especially those who take solace in a religious faith. In this prejudice, my father has impressive company. The great psychologist Sigmund Freud regarded religion as an illusion without a future. But like all revolutionaries, Freud could not live without his own reservoir of faith, which was science. Human progress was his creed.

Whether they are secularists like my father and Freud, or religious zealots like Mohammed Atta, those who believe we can become masters of our fates think they know more than Pascal. But in their search for truth, where do they imagine they have gone that he did not go before them? What do they think they know that Pascal did not? Their bravado is only a mask for the inevitable defeat that is our common lot, an inverse mirror of their human need.

Like Mohammed Atta, my father was an ineffectual man thwarted in his earthly desires. When he was still young, he gave up his ambitions, and resigned himself to a life without them. But in his imagination he knew no such limits. The hope he no longer had for himself he invested in others. Even though my father prided himself on being a practical man without illusions, he shared with Mohammed Atta and his believers an impossible dream. Their dream was to change the world. What Mohammed Atta and my father wanted was an escape from this life.

If his views had been described to him this way, my father would have rejected the link to theological illusions. He felt as superior to the religious revolutionaries who shared his dreams as they did to secular radicals like him. But while he disdained their God and their paradise in heaven, he never gave up their belief in miracles of faith.

My father's prophet was Karl Marx, who was himself descended from a long line of rabbis. Like my father, Marx disdained the religion of his ancestors, regarding it as the comforting myths of weak-minded men. But the icon he chose for his secular faith was a mythical figure all the same. His hero was Prometheus, the pagan who stole fire from the gods and brought a piece of heaven to earth.

Like Freud, Marx regarded the belief in heaven as a cry of impotence, a memory from the childhood of the race when men were tormented by forces of nature they could not understand. To cope with their predicament they conjured powers that were divine and would look after them, and keep them safe. Marx knew the divinities they worshipped were only reflections of themselves on whom they projected powers that might one day be theirs. Marx's revolutionary message to humanity was this: *You shall be as gods.*

For Marx, religious belief was not a consolation for human unhappiness but its cause. The God that men worshipped appeared to them as the embodiment of their hope. But Marx knew that their deity was only a tribal totem whose worship made them passive and denied them their due. There were no unanswerable questions or unattainable powers that determined human fate. Marx was so confident of this truth that he summed up his conclusion in a single sentence: "All mysteries, which lead to mysticism, find their rational solution in human practice." Marx's revelation was this: The fire is not in heaven; it is in *you.* Human beings could achieve their liberation by worshipping themselves instead of gods. This was a flattery so great that it changed the world.

In Marx's telling, religious faith was not a passage to heaven but a passion of the condemned. "Religion is the sigh of the oppressed creature, the heart of a heartless world, and the soul of a soulless condition," he wrote; "it is the opium of the oppressed." Thus Marx inverted the martyr's hope. In Marx's gospel, the dream of a heavenly paradise is no longer the aspiration to transcend human fate. It is the snare that seduces us into accepting our unhappy condition. The dream of heaven is a pitiful perversion of humanity's desire to liberate itself and make the world one. Marx's call to revolution is this: Give up the dream of a paradise in heaven in order to create a heaven on earth. In the book he mockingly titled *The Holy Family,* he declared, "The abolition of religion as the illusory happiness of the people is required for their real happiness."

These words stand Marx's proclamation on its proverbial head and show how pathetically human his prophecy was. Having dismissed religion and fantastic dreams, he succumbs to them himself. Having claimed that the world could not be saved by religion, he insists it will be saved by abolishing religion. In place of the old redemption through the grace of God, the revolutionary offers a secular salvation. In place of the Final Judgment and a world made holy through divine intervention, Marx promises Social Justice, a world redeemed through the actions of ordinary men.

Like Islamic radicals pursuing their goal of God's law on earth, Marx drew a line between the House of Faith and the House of War, between those who were chosen for the progressive mission and the reactionaries whose removal is necessary to transform the world.

My father was a decent man who was not prepared to harm others, even in the service of his radical faith, let alone murder innocents as Mohammed Atta did. But along with millions of decent progressive souls, my father abetted those who did just that. Progressives looked the other way and then endorsed the murder of untold innocents for the same reason that Mohammed Atta and the Islamic martyrs did: to make the new world possible. Their desire for judgment in this life was so strong it inspired them to believe that if enough of the guilty were punished, they could actually produce one.

I understand Pascal's religion. I understand his anxious bewilderment at a life of no consequence. I understand his hope for a personal redemption, and his search for an answer. But I no longer understand my father's faith, his belief that men alone without divine intervention can transform the world in which they find themselves and create a paradise on earth.

Some may regard these speculations as unreasonable. How can a man invoke his father in the same sentence as Mohammed Atta? My answer is, *How not?* Was

Mohammed Atta not flesh and blood; if you pricked him did he not bleed? What did Mohammed Atta hope for but a better world; and what progressive soul does not wish for that?

Like my father, I once thought I knew the answers to unanswerable questions, and allowed myself to dream impossible dreams. But one day these dreams brought tragedy to my door, and I put away the illusion for good. Whoever asks how Mohammed Atta's awful deed can be linked to decent people has not understood the deed, or who they themselves are. Ask yourself this: Up to the last act of Mohammed Atta's life, would he have been judged an evil person? No one who actually knew him thinks so.

The act that ended Mohammed's life and thousands of innocent others was surely evil. But except for the terrible deed itself, there is not an inconsiderate gesture attached to his memory. He appears to have been an ordinary man who was seduced into committing a great crime in the name of a greater good. Is this not the most common theme of the human tragedies of our time?

Ordinary lives will encompass selfishness and greed and the occasional ability to inflict harm without compunction. That is our human portion. But the capacity for dedicated evil is a rarer quality. The Pharaonic masters of our suffering are a small current in the human sea. Decent multitudes must swell behind them to create the tides that shape history's monstrous results. Many epic crimes have been supported by common fear, but more are driven by desperate hope. What the worshippers of history's murderers seek is justification for a life. And for a life that is not this one.

Both Marx and Mohammed agreed that history is the story of men who serve false gods, and liberation a leap into the kingdom of truth, where men will be both free and blessed. But how did they propose to get to such a place through the agency of ordinary human beings?

Martin Amis is one of Saul Bellow's literary disciples. In a book he called *Koba the Dread,* Amis casts an artist's eye on Joseph Stalin, the Marxist liberator and my father's hero, who attempted to engineer the future on an epic scale. Amis's portrait draws on the witness of Stalin's contemporaries, among whom we find this instructive note: "[Stalin] is unhappy at not being able to convince everyone that he is greater than everyone."

This is the diary comment of Nikolai Bukharin, a Bolshevik leader and intimate of Stalin's, and an imminent victim of the great man's dementia. In happier days before his fall, Bukharin had romped with Stalin on *dacha* lawns and had once even carried the nation's savior on his back.

Bukharin jotted down this diary entry during the blood-soaked days that history knows as the Great Purge, which was Stalin's campaign to eradicate enemies of the revolution and rivals to himself. In a two-year period beginning in 1936, Bukharin's playful friend ordered the executions of a million citizens of the Soviet state, mostly members of his own party, often his closest associates and friends. Among the dead were acolytes who had promoted him as the "Father of the Peoples" and a "genius of mankind," and artists who had praised him as a human god. The victims of his terror included family intimates, their wives and children. His own wife committed suicide in horror at what he had done.

As the procession of executions accelerated, the pathetic Bukharin was desperate to explain why Stalin would destroy those so near to him, fearing correctly that he would be next. Even as he contemplated his doom at the hands of a maniac, Bukharin felt a tug of sympathy for a man whose intentions he had shared. "This unhappiness of his may be his most human trait, perhaps the only human trait in him. But what is rather not human, but something of the devil, is that because of this unhappiness he cannot help taking revenge on people, on all people, but especially on those who are in any way better or higher than he."

Of course, Bukharin was wrong. This very envy and the cruel desire for revenge that accompanied it were Joseph Stalin's most human traits. These are the passions that produced the great leveling called "socialism," which until his moment of truth had been Bukharin's own.

Amis notes that Stalin, who murdered more than twenty million people to create the workers' paradise and make himself immortal, had two famous comments about the mortality of others. The first was this: "Death solves all problems—no man, no problem." The second: "The death of one man is a tragedy, the death of millions a statistic."

Not all the plans that men devise to find a way out of history turn on the elimination of social classes or the establishment of religious law. Hitler's idea was to get rid of the Jews. As a result of his plan, most of my family lineages end in 1939, the year I was born. I can trace my origins back through my father's father and my mother's grandfather, but the trail stops there. The communities of Eastern Europe, of Moravia and Ukraine from which my ancestors came, ended up in the gas chambers and are now erased.

Even if Hitler had not launched his Final Solution, I still would probably have a hard time tracing my family's steps. This is because well before Hitler my forebears had found a way—or so they hoped—to escape their Jewish fate. Instead of embracing the congregation of Abraham, they abandoned both tribe and faith and became "internationalists." As progressives they joined a movement that also proposed to "solve the Jewish problem," but benevolently, by turning humanity into one happy family and making the Jews "like everyone else." As socialists, they set out to eradicate the very sources of human division and conflict—property, classes and national identities—as though history could be abolished by human decree.

My father was one of the millions of decent souls who believed in Stalin as the people's leader, and counted on him to rescue them from their benighted state. But if you were to ask them, not a single one of these enlightened souls would concede any connection between their personal anxieties and their social agendas. They would be repelled by the idea that the progressive fantasy is really the expression of a religious desire.

To the devoted, the source of human misery cannot be located in a deficiency of self, let alone the wish to escape it. That would diminish the suffering and make human beings responsible for themselves. To the revolutionary, the source of this misery can only be a corruption in "society," a fault in the world that other men have made. The revolutionary mission is to cleanse the world of this corruption and its agents, and reverse the human Fall. The secular purification of the world has a name: *social justice*. It is the *sharia* of political faith.

Marx explained the difference between the revolutionary desire for social justice and all other attempts at social reform: "[The revolutionary class] claims no particular right, because it claims no particular wrong, since wrong in general is perpetrated against it." In other words, injustice is not a specific dysfunction. The very order of the world is wrong and the revolutionary's task is to make it right. The language is secular, but the aim is no less comprehensive than converting the infidels or purging them from the face of the earth. For believers the creation of a just world is the end of history, and therefore its beginning. Their vision is total, and nothing escapes it. Because it is both the beginning and the end, the mission to create a new world justifies anything. And everything.

In his book about the hell that progressives like Bukharin had constructed in Russia, Martin Amis included the diary entry of a factory-school worker named Stepan Podlubny. For his loyalty to the cause, Stepan had been made a "Sentinel of the Revolution."

His task was to inform on workers who failed to observe the revolutionary code. The year was 1932, and the collectivization of agriculture had already begun. In his diary, Stepan recorded feelings he could not reveal without putting his own life in danger.

He was concerned about his mother, who had been sentenced to eight years in a concentration camp for concealing information. The incriminating knowledge related to herself. Stepan's mother had been a kulak whose family property was confiscated to make way for the liberated future. Her son could not believe the judgment that the socialist authorities had pronounced on his mother. "They consider her a danger to society. You'd think they caught a bandit, but even bandits get lighter sentences than that," he wrote. "Is this the end of justice on earth?"

With this question, Stepan had come face to face with the revolutionary truth. Consider how the effort to redeem the future begins by making identity a crime. Who was Stepan's mother? How did she acquire the status that condemned her? This was the question that Stepan could not answer and it was one the court could not ask. The court's mission was revolutionary; its mandate was not to understand the past but to condemn it.

We come into this world unequal and each follows a unique path to the seat of judgment. What is justice, if it cannot recognize our human uniqueness? How can there be a *social* justice that is not an offense to who and what we are?

The revolution has no time to pause over the individual and his truth, nor could it do so without losing its way. To become socially just, the world must obey the revolutionary rule. Because revolutionaries cannot respect what lies outside the rule and remain revolutionaries, they are led to statements like this: "We must rid ourselves once and for all of the Quaker-Papist babble about the sanctity of human life." These are the words of the Bolshevik Trotsky, who along with his son and his friends and comrades was eventually murdered in the revolution's name.

In another passage of his book, Martin Amis prints the testimony of a Nazi doctor who was interviewed in the aftermath of World War II. The doctor had participated in Hitler's attempt at a Final Solution to the problem of the Jews, experimenting on the condemned and assisting the radicals in their genocidal program to purify the race. The interview with the doctor was conducted in sight of the ovens in which his victims' corpses had been disposed. Pointing to the chimneys that were now smokeless, the interviewer asked, "How can you reconcile *that* with your oath as a doctor? The Nazi

answered: 'Of course, I am a doctor and I want to preserve life. And out of respect for human life I would
remove a gangrenous appendix from a diseased body.
The Jew is the gangrenous appendix in the body of
mankind.'"

Here is the paradox of all dreams of a redeemed
future. The more beautiful the dream, the more necessary the crime.

Pascal understood the human pain from which epic
ambitions arise: "Man would be great and sees that he
is little; would be happy and sees that he is miserable;
would be perfect and sees that he is full of imperfec-
tions; would be the object of the love and esteem of
men, and sees that his faults merit only their aversion
and contempt. The embarrassment wherein he finds
himself produces in him the most unjust and criminal
passions imaginable, for he conceives a mortal hatred
against that truth which blames him and convinces him
of his faults."

Self-loathing is the secret revolutionary passion.
Every transformer of mankind is inspired to destroy a
world that condemns him. Every revolutionary despises
the other who tells him who he is. It is the unbelievers
who provide the mirror in which the truth confronts
him: the peasant who wants a piece of the earth; the

Jew who triumphs despite a defective birth; the infidel who finds pleasure in a world that is dust. To the radical soul, it is this that is finally unbearable.

While Pascal was an agnostic of the intellect, he was a believer of the heart. He recognized that his condition was hopeless and that only a divinity could heal his mortal sickness and make him whole. Because science offered no answers to his questions, he trusted in the God of Abraham to provide what no ordinary mortal can. Pascal was a realist of faith. He drew a line between the sacred and the profane, respecting the gulf that separates this world from the next. Therefore, he did not presume to achieve his own salvation in this world, or anyone else's.

Not so the social redeemers. They cannot live with themselves or the fault in creation, and therefore are at war with both. Because they are miserable themselves they cannot abide the happiness of others. To escape their suffering they seek judgment on all, the rectification that will take them home. If they do not believe in a God, they summon others to act as gods. If they believe in God, they do not trust His justice but arrange their own. In either case, the consequence of their passion is the same catastrophe. This is because the devil they hate is in themselves and their sword of vengeance is wielded by inhabitants of the very hell they wish to escape.

There is no redemption in this life. Generation after generation, we transmit our faults and pass on our sins. From parents to children, we create the world in our own image. And no power can stop us. Every life is an injustice. And no one can fix it. We are born and we die. If there is no God to rescue us, we are nothing.

FOUR
Being Here

At innumerable points in the trajectory my life has taken, there have been turnings where my fate would have been irrevocably altered, had I but changed the simplest decision and set my foot on a different path. It is a fact I reflect on often, but like everyone else can't do anything about.

One July day in the summer of 1994, I set out to meet a woman I didn't know in a place I had never been, with intentions that were incompletely disclosed. At the time, I was living in the marina apartment and working on a memoir in which I intended to trace the footsteps of my receding life. The encounter came unexpectedly through a friend who asked me to provide advice on a medical matter to someone in need. As an afterthought or perhaps to pique my interest, the friend had also mentioned that the patient, whose name was April, was a beautiful woman.

The counsel I was being asked to provide concerned a virus-induced ailment known as chronic fatigue syndrome, a malady I had been stricken with years before. The condition was one normally diagnosed as "incurable" and, when you thought about it, was almost a metaphor for middle age. A poignant aspect of this case was the youth of the victim herself.

The symptoms of the illness were a brain perpetually fogged and an immense tiredness that hooded the eyes, suffusing the limbs with a languorous indolence from which I felt I would never wake up. I went through a summer in this state and then a winter, and then another, shuffling along sunlit sidewalks like a sea tortoise encrusted with time, until I began to wonder if this was what I had finally become.

Frustrated with the prognoses of doctors who prepared me for a permanently reduced life, I consulted "New Age" practitioners of the healing arts who assured me that treatment was possible. Eventually, I came under the care of a Belgian doctor who had a license in acupuncture, and a reputation for effecting cures. He stuck me with needles, injected a Chinese serum into my "points," pumped me with amino acids and adjusted my diet. He also encouraged the only exercise I could manage, which was the long walks I took at a reptilian pace.

The virus was affected by heat and dampness, and on days that were overcast and muggy I surrendered to its superior force. In time, the syndrome established its own rhythm of ebb and flow, allowing me to work in the intervals when its virulence relented. In those hours, I resumed my half-life and doggedly followed the regimen that the doctor prescribed, dragging my shell along glacial miles while awaiting the miracle that would return the spring to my step.

My recovery was slow and the setbacks recurrent, but it did come. When I finally revived, I was unable to determine whether it was the remedies that had worked or whether I owed my return to the healing powers of the body itself. Nonetheless, I routinely praised the man who had looked after me when I needed encouragement and help. This was how, on a hot summer's day, I found myself headed for Brea, California, to meet a woman I had never met before.

The pretext for the trip was an appointment I had at a venue in Costa Mesa, which was actually along the hypotenuse of a triangle twenty-five miles to the west. In our phone conversation I had mentioned that I would be "in the neighborhood" and it might be a convenient time to drop by with an armful of medical texts. En route, I lost my way and became so frustrated with the effort to get back on course that I began to think seriously about turning around and going home. Why was I pursuing a stranger like this, at *my* age?

The work address she had given me was a plastic surgeon's office, where she provided skin care for patients who came to have their faces reshaped. This odd but very modern idea became the subject of my thoughts during the boredom of the drive, and led to some familiar reflections. How much of ourselves is finally in our bodies? What is reality and what appearance?

These were ancient questions that I had first encountered as a young man in school. Plato and his followers believed the flesh was incidental to our being and that ideas were the only reality. The eyes, he thought, were the windows to the soul, as though in the darkness behind retina and iris lay the goodness, beauty and truth of who we are. It was an interesting suggestion, but ultimately unconvincing. How much do we see of others when we see them, especially for the first time?

When I arrived, April appeared (gloriously I thought) in her white smock, more blonde than I had imagined. A generous smile welcomed me as she approached, and I felt my head lower in unaccustomed shyness. Even as we slipped into a patter of introductions, it occurred to me that the romantic angle I had devised for the plot was not going to work. I thought: this woman's life is so different from mine that if I had arrived from the planet Mars, the distance between us could not have been greater.

In an attempt to collect myself, I began thumbing the pages of one of the tracts my doctor had written as guides through the bogs of chronic fatigue.

Nervously, I began to read aloud to her, selecting choice advice from the open text. I was encouraged when she seemed more intrigued by my fluster than by the doctor's good counsel. But when I asked her to dinner she begged off, saying she wasn't feeling well and didn't have the energy for an evening. Had my intentions been purer, her explanation would have seemed perfectly reasonable. As it was, I thought: *that is the end of that.*

However, as is often the case when we try to predict our futures, I was mistaken. From our first steps continuing to our last, we see through the glass darkly. Our lives are a series of blind encounters, and no surgeon, however expert in his craft, can alter that. We can never know where the paths we follow may lead, and we cannot take a single step back. And no power available to us can change this fact.

I don't know why April responded to the calls I made to her after I left, or why she agreed to see me again, or why when we had become familiar and my lips reached for hers, she wanted to receive them. Or how an improbable romance bloomed as it did.

But then I am not alone in my ignorance of such important things. "God knows," Saul Bellow remarked late in his life, "why we are drawn to others and become attached to them." As if to provide an answer (or to illustrate there was none), Bellow recalled how Proust, the novelist of love, once said that he was "often attracted to people who had something in them of a hawthorn hedge in bloom." Was April, then, an iris blonder than spring, as she seemed to me now? Perhaps Proust would have understood the attraction.

As I continued to reflect on how strange we were to each other, the idea became increasingly attractive. Perhaps there was an advantage for us in the strangeness itself. Experience had taught me that one of the chief obstacles in maintaining such bonds lay in taking the other for granted. It occurred to me that our distances would prompt us to be mindful of the gap and encourage us to keep the other in sight.

Our trysts took place on my turf in the marina. Several days a week she would travel the forty-mile distance along the freeways to have dinner with me and spend the night. I didn't think much about this pattern of our meetings, because the arrangement suited me. But whenever I did, I assumed it was somehow for her convenience. Perhaps she found my apartment, which fronted the water, more congenial than her subdivision with its thick summer heat.

Our romance was well into its fourth month when she revealed the reason behind the routine. This was the fact that she was the mother of a boy of eight, whose name was John, and whose existence she had hidden.

By design, she had kept our romance at my end of the woods, so to speak, in order to conceal our relationship from him and theirs from me.

As she told me this, I noted her hesitation, and read into it several folds of concern. Our mutual passion had grown unexpectedly and she now realized that the penalty for her deception might be more serious than she had bargained. It was possible that a man of my years might not want the burdens of a second family so late in life.

She could have saved herself the worry. Even before she began explaining, I understood that hiding her son was a way to keep from me an intimate and vulnerable part of herself when our relationship was still fresh. Far from alarming me, her secret was reassuring. The lengths she had gone to protect her child's love told me how careful she would be with mine. I had already given her my own hostage. Who can hurt you more than someone who has your heart?

Sigmund Freud was bent on returning us to the animal kingdom. To account for my attraction to April, Freud would have reached for a biological function, and explained it as my plot to stay alive. "The union of numerous cells into one vital connection is a means to the prolongation of their span of life," he asserted in a famous text. "Conjugation, the temporary mingling of two unicellular entities, has a preservative and rejuvenating effect on both." April, then, was my rejuvenating mate.

Beyond the Pleasure Principle, which contains these observations, is Freud's effort to understand the "death wish," a concept he based on the idea that we are drawn to what we fear. According to Freud's text, organic instincts are conservative and regressive, seeking to reinstate a previous condition. This was like a commentary on my father's observation: From the beginning of life we instinctively long for the end.

But why *instinctively?* Why not logically? If life is a meaningless ripple of empty space, why not get it over with, and sooner rather than later? Isn't it survival that requires an instinct and an explanation? This question itself reveals what a mystery life is, even to those who believe we are no more than bodies and imagine it is a puzzle that science can solve.

In thinking that we are no more than the cells that compose us, contemporary materialists display an even greater arrogance than Freud's. The tissue of the human brain has a hundred billion neurons connected by a hundred trillion synapses, but evolutionary psychologists are convinced they can figure out what makes us tick. "Every emotion and thought gives off physical signals," writes one, "and the new technologies for detecting them are so accurate that they can literally read a person's mind.... Neural network modelers have begun to show how the building blocks of mental computation, such as storing and retrieving a pattern, can be implemented in neural circuitry. And when the brain dies, the person goes out of existence."

And how, exactly, would he know?

No scientific argument, no matter how persuasive, could convince me that the love I feel is simply a matter of biological pulls. At my age the electrical pulses don't account for nearly as much as when I was twenty. They have been overtaken by the impulses of the soul, which, no matter how old you get, can still grab you, and make you sit up and listen.

When April and I had been together for ten years, she said this: "When you die, I tell myself I'll be seeing you spiritually some day again. I don't know how I would live with the thought of you gone, if I didn't believe that. I don't know how people who have no belief in God manage. It's a sad way to carry your heart through life."

But she knew I did just that. She said, "You need to respect God more. He's been good to you. When you came out of the operating room you were so handsome and your skin was magical, there was a glow on you. I knew that someone, maybe your Grandma Rose, or your mom was looking out for you." And then she said, "You have a mission. Most people are like me and don't. But you have a mission. God is protecting you."

It is a privilege to be loved. It can almost make you a believer, even if believing is not in you from the beginning. You give, and if you are fortunate what you give comes back, and it comes back in ways you would never have imagined.

I could not easily dismiss this idea of a grace unseen. I knew I had taken risks that others avoided and had escaped unharmed. I had been felled by a cancer and was still around to talk about it. But what was the mission that might cause God to look out for me? Why would the God of the Jews take a hand in the affairs of one of His children in any case? The biblical point was that the Creator gave us free will to determine our fates. Why would He intervene to change mine?

I did have a mission at one time that tragedy overwhelmed and brought to an end. As a result, I no longer shared my father's dream of an earthly redemption. I had come to see such dreams as a vortex of destruction and had become an adversary of those who kept them alive. It was my way of atoning for what I had done. This was the mission to which April referred.

But while I took pleasure in her romance, I could not flatter myself to think that a providential eye was looking out for me and shaping my ends. This was the very illusion I had escaped. The personal dream of every revolutionary is to be at the center of creation and the renewal of the world. What I had learned in my life was that we were not at the center of anything, except our own insignificance. There was nothing indispensable about me; or about anyone.

The wars of the social redeemers were as old as Babel and would go on forever. The dreamers would go on building towers to heaven, and just as inexorably they would come crashing to earth. Some would take to heart the lessons of the fall, but most would fail to notice them, or care. Inspired by those who preceded them and innocent of their crimes, an unending cycle of generations would repeat what they had done. The terrible suffering of innocent and guilty alike would continue without end. The Prophet Mohammed would beget the disciple Atta; the prophet Marx, my father. Others would follow them, and nothing I could do or say would change it.

The summons I answered was more modest by far than any mission that God might notice. It was to bear witness to what I had learned. Perhaps hearing my story, another, as innocent as I had been, would take heed. For myself, I needed to remember what I had learned through pain, and to honor my debt. My mission was as much for myself as for anyone else. It was about wrestling with the most powerful and pernicious of all human follies, which is the desire to stifle truth in the name of hope.

Here is why you cannot change the world: Because we—all six billion of us—create it. We do so individually and relentlessly and in every generation. We shape it as monarchs in our homes and masters beyond, when we cannot even master ourselves. Every breeder of new generations is a stranger to his mate and a mystery to himself. Every offspring is a self-creator who learns through rebellion and contrition, through injury and error, and frequently not at all. This is the root cause that makes us who and what we are—the good, the bad, the demented, the wise, the benevolent and the brute. We are creatures blind and ignorant, stumbling helplessly through a puff of time.

The future is a work of prejudice and malice inextricably bound with generosity and hope. It is carried out now and forever under the terrible anarchy of freedom that God has imposed on his children and will not take back. This world is created every day by us at odds with each other, and over and over. It is irrevocably broken into billions of fragments, bits of human unhappiness and earthly frustration. And no one can fix it.

In my life's journey I have acquired a public persona. As a result, strangers sometimes approach me bearing images of a self, lost long ago. In a recent spring, I spoke at a university in Connecticut, whose name I have forgotten. When my talk was over, a compact man with Irish curls and a snow-white beard came up to introduce himself: "It's me, Johnny O'Brien," he volunteered, foreseeing that I would not be able to recognize him. All at once, the eye of memory began daubing color into place, rusting the locks and deepening the freckles that time had faded, until I was able to identify the youth who had stood in front of me in the lines arranged by size place at the elementary school we both attended half a century before.

With the recognition came old feelings that reminded me of the fondness and frustration with which I had approached him when we were both so young. I recalled my desire to reach out to him and be his friend and also how we never did become close. When we had talked for a while, I asked him how he had regarded me then. "You were frightening," he said. "I was twelve and just trying to figure out who I was and what it was all about. But you already knew." Of course, I did; I was already embarked on my father's mission. "You had a certainty and a purpose," John continued, "that was daunting in someone so inexperienced and young. It was as though you knew what to think about everything, about who you were and where you were going. I sensed in you an indefinable contempt for those who were too ignorant to see these truths. It was clear to me that it was impossible for someone unanointed with such knowledge to get near you. So I gave up trying."

John's father was a New York fireman with an eighth-grade education, an immigrant who wanted his son to make good in a new country where making good was a possible dream. John was able to fulfill his father's ambition, becoming a classics professor and writing a noted book about Alexander the Great, with sources in seven languages. The life of his subject even resonated with his own, since Alexander was a man driven by the ambition to surpass his father. While able to dominate others, however, Alexander lost the battle with his own demon, alcohol. In John's view, the god Dionysius was the "invisible enemy" who eventually brought down the greatest figure of the classical age. As John told it, Alexander's story was that of a man who had conquered the world but in the end could not conquer himself.

The certainty that frightened John when he saw it in me was my own Dionysian nemesis, my wine of denial fermented in the vineyard of my father's dreams. At twelve, I was already intoxicated by my father's mission, pursuing his hope and earnestly recruiting others to follow. In my memoir, *Radical Son,* I related how this fantasy undid me, and how tragedy had finally bled its arrogant presence from my soul.

Small as I was compared to Alexander, I had made a conquest of self that he could not. The advantage I had over the undefeated hero was failure; the fall I had taken, my saving grace. In my memoir I wrote: "The disorder of my life—which I understood to be a disorder of myself—allowed me to see for the first time. I began asking questions I had never thought to ask. *Why am I doing this? What do I want? What do I need?* As the life I had so carefully and purposefully constructed disintegrated before my eyes, I realized that I didn't really know. The chaos I found myself in had shifted my vision. The very sense of failure, of bottomless defeat, proved a grace. For the first time in my life, I could not address others from a moral high ground. I was no longer busy bringing them the good news. It was I who needed help. For the first time in my life, I wanted to listen."

Discussing fathers and sons with a professor of classics, along with the intimacy between suffering and knowledge, made my conversation with John O'Brien seem very old. What could be more Oedipal or more obvious than that we must be humbled in order to see?

A few months after our first encounter, April and I traveled to Santa Fe—the City of Holy Faith—to pay a visit to the doctor who had helped me through my illness. The air is thinner in the high desert and the light whiter and more intense than anywhere else. It is a combination that creates weightlessness in the head and the soul. The result is an environment not recommended for heart cases, but seductive for artists and lovers. I had planned the trip in the hope that my doctor could improve April's health, but when we got there, he failed to inspire her faith in his homeopathic remedies, and our medical agenda was thus concluded.

The first night we bedded down in a motel designed like a Spanish inn with the rooms furnished in dark oak. Soon after falling asleep we were roused by a banging at the door and the noise of human voices. It was April who lurched to consciousness first. "Someone's breaking in," she said, her voice a blade of panic in the darkness. I was on my feet instantly, grabbing one of the heavy chairs and brandishing it lancelike—my knight in armor to her damsel in distress. *"Who's there?"* I barked menacingly, still leaden with sleep.

Just then April flicked on the light. Its glare
exposed my nakedness and revealed that I was facing
a blank wall. The noise we had taken for intruders at
the door was a drunken party in the neighboring suite
and my chair still risibly aloft was fending off phan-
toms. Seeing me so preposterously poised, April burst
into laughter, rendering my situation immediately
worse. But just as quickly she relented. "How romantic," she said, without a trace of irony. This was the
first of many lighthearted interludes of intimacy
together, which I already hoped would carry us to the
end of time.

In the next days, we planned to visit friends and
explore the desert landscapes. Driving north past cac-
tus plains and red earth mesas, we arrived in the city
of Taos, a luminous place where Georgia O'Keefe had
made canvases bloom and D. H. Lawrence had written a story about a woman who fell in love with the
sun. We stopped there to tour an adobe church, which
seemed haunted by the spirits of dead padres and con-
quistadors, and then continued our drive. The road
took us up through the Sangre de Cristo Mountains,
where the escarpments were a deep hunter's green and
the crests haloed in blue mists that made the range
appear as sanctified as its name.

My friends had built a lovers' retreat in the high
country, but (as we were to discover) had become

ensnared in the web of a doomed marriage instead. The wife had hoped to find respite in the mountains from the turmoil of her life in California's Silicon Valley, where her wealthy husband was a corporate leader. She was restless there (and indeed wherever she was) and had persuaded him to buy the isolated nook in the Cristo range to create their mountain idyll.

It was a location she had selected long before she met him, when she was a student without means and could hardly have dreamed of the house she eventually built. With funds he provided, she had overseen the construction of a two-story villa with great wooden beams and fieldstone carapaces. The imposing edifice made a fitting crown to the romance that had failed. "I placed each stone in that wall and designed every room in the house," the wife told me bitterly when it was no longer hers.

Alongside the main structure there was a stream, which they had blocked, dredging the bed to form an artificial lake that rippled gracefully in the mountain wind. A canopy of clouds drifted listlessly overhead, and in the pale light, the unquiet surface of the water acquired a metallic sheen and a serenity that seemed otherworldly. Long before her marriage, my friend had adopted the Hindu faith in an effort to calm her unsatisfied desires and lift the veil of unhappiness that had shrouded her from youth. When the knot was tied, she led her husband onto her spiritual path, encouraging him to invest millions in his adopted creed.

On the verge of the lake, she had built a meditation room out of redwood planks and fitted it with a window facing the water, where the melancholy light could inspire her reflections. When it was finished, her guru came to visit and bless the site. Daily, beside the magical tide, the wife meditated on Maya, the illusion of the world she had created. But its loss devastated her all the same.

It is our common lot to share our joys but be alone in our sorrows, whose labyrinths no other can enter. April and I took in my friend's misery, considered it, and returned to our private delights. In the rooms that had been decorated with elaborate care, in the gardens cultivated with affection, we reveled in our own Maya, exploring the life we had begun together and relishing the wonder at where we would go next.

I already knew I loved April and hoped that her feelings were as tender toward me. When our Santa Fe trip was over, we headed back to Los Angeles and to our solitary homes, a constant separation I looked forward to ending. But I kept my counsel and did not reveal in so many words the feelings I harbored. It would be months before I would be able to do so, and more than a year before I would ask her to share a house with me so that we would return always to the same address. Another would pass before I felt free to ask her to be my wife.

It was April who was skeptical of verbal commitments and who imposed this discipline, making clear that too bold a declaration would be suspect if it were based on experience too slight to trust. She was as cautious in these matters as I frequently was not. I yielded to her restraints, keeping my desire to marry her secret until patience had earned it a gravity she would respect.

Was this deception? Only if her reasons for requiring the caution were identical to mine in resisting it. Only if the judgments each of us make proceed along similar axes to similar results. But the experiences that shape our judgments are never the same. We are alone in our choices. No matter how intimately we know each other, or for how long, we will always be strangers in this.

When the waiting was over, my instinct was proven right. It has been ten years now that we have been together since the day we first met. But I will never know whether the wait she imposed was necessary to achieve this desired result. It is the same for all the decisions that define us. We do not get to retrace our steps and test the choices that we make, or to see where others would have led.

As the marriage day approached, I searched for some ceremonial words to say to my bride and was reminded of a phrase from a play I had seen as a young man. I have remembered this line (whether accurately or not doesn't really matter) for nearly half a century. It is a comment by one of the characters on how the strange and uncertain circumstances of our lives cause us to grope in the dark and to feel ourselves lucky when we actually find our way. "Sometimes," the character remarks, "you have to go a long way out of the way to come a short way correctly."

Perhaps I was impressed by this sentiment because it seemed to justify the mistakes I had made along my way, which deflected me from what had been my intended path. The rationale is a familiar one. We constantly tell ourselves that something we regret and cannot explain "happened for a reason." But did it? How often have we used the phrase not because we can say with certainty that something did happen for a reason, but rather to comfort ourselves for opportunities we have missed or tragedies we cannot comprehend?

There is a reason that we yearn to make sense of lost time. We are looking for reassurance that God is taking care of us, and that it is death finally, and not life, that is the dream.

It occurred to me that in counseling patience, April had become my tutor in a lesson that had eluded me all my life. Her caution was the reason it was her first marriage and my impulsive lack why it was not mine. I knew she was anxious about the fact that she was not my first wife and decided to let her know that it was actually a bond—however implausible—that connected us.

Thinking of the missteps I had made on my way to our altar, I recalled the line from the play, and said, "We pay for our sins, but we are not always rewarded for what we do right. Today I am rewarded. Unexpectedly, undeservedly; but rewarded all the same. I am grateful to have been given this day a woman with so good a heart and so generous a soul. In this moment I see that my whole life has been a long going out of the way to come a short way to you."

Saul Bellow had five marriages. In his novel *Humboldt's Gift,* he created an alter ego with similar bad luck named Charlie Citrine, whose wife had left him for another man and filed a ruinous lawsuit against him. While telling a friend about his marital trials Citrine makes the following observation concerning his case: "It keeps me in touch with the facts of life. It's been positively enlightening."

"How so?"

"Well, I realize how universal the desire to injure your fellow man is."

It is tempting to dismiss this judgment as the self-serving cynicism of a habitual defendant. But an honest reader will recognize in it a theme of all our divorces, marital and otherwise. Each time an intimacy comes to an end and ardor turns to revenge, we are given a glimpse of the abyss that lies under the surface of all our peace.

Our innocence is amazed that someone who has loved us can want to destroy us. But why should this be remarkable? The reversal of passion expresses our vulnerability and is the rage at its betrayal. We are rootless and alone and threatened with extinction. In this circumstance, survival is our consummate narcissism, denial our first defense. Is there a limit to what human beings will do to save themselves when they believe their backs are to the wall? Will they not lie, steal, cheat, even kill? When we think we have no alternative—a conclusion reached easily enough—what is unfair and injurious to me, will seem like perfect justice to you.

A rabbi named Joseph Telushkin has written a popular text called *The Ten Commandments of Character,* whose aim is to offer readers "essential advice for living an honorable, ethical and honest life." The rabbi's

Third Commandment tells us to "Treat All People with Kindness and with the Understanding That They, Like You, Are 'Made in God's Image.'" To prove the wisdom of this commandment, Rabbi Telushkin asks, "Would terrorists plant bombs in public places if they had not first blinded themselves to the fact that the people they kill and maim are, like themselves and their families, created in God's image?" The rabbi answers: "All instances of evil—from the Holocaust to the humiliation of a single person—have in common the perpetrator's unwillingness to see the image of God in each human being." In other words, understand that God is in every one of His children and you will harm none.

But is this so? Is it possible that when Mohammed Atta drove his plane into the North Tower of the World Trade Center he did not believe with his whole heart that Allah had created each and every one of his victims? Of course he did. That was why he killed them: to fulfill God's plan.

Was not Mohammed Atta himself created in God's image? If he had survived his own atrocity should he then have been treated with kindness and respect? Was not Satan created in God's image? The Prince of Evil was God's favorite angel before his fall from grace. And what are we but fallen creatures ourselves?

It is folly to imagine that terror can be exorcised by saccharine homilies like Rabbi Telushkin's. You could invert the meaning of his commandment and do better: *Do not aspire to see God in yourself, for pride goeth before a fall.* The fall of Satan—and of Adam—sprang from their dissatisfaction with the world as it is, from their *desire to be like God.*

The evil of this world is not caused by ignorance of the good or failure to appreciate the holiness of human life. It is caused by the black hole that lies at the bottom of every human soul.

What I had learned through the most painful experiences of my life was to pay attention to the differences. It was a lesson at odds with the moral teachings that had come down to us across the millennia. All the prophets—Moses, Jesus, Buddha, the Hindu gurus—have taught an opposite truth: that however different we may look and act, we are one. High and low, strong and weak, virtuous and sinful, we are all incarnations of the same divine spirit. Underneath our various skins, all are kin. "There but for the grace of God, go I."

But do we?

"Treat a stranger as you would be treated. Love thy neighbor as thyself." These commandments are said to sum up the moral law. But is it really prudent advice to put our trust in strangers, or to love our enemies as ourselves? Would we counsel our children to do so?

Do we really regard ourselves as one with rapists and murderers? Or should we? It is true that the capacity for evil is in our nature, and this makes us kin. But I feel no kinship with those who can cut a human life short without remorse; with terrorists who target the innocent for death; or with adults who torment children for sexual thrills. I suspect I am not alone in this.

In the realm of the spirit, it is easier to slide a mile back than to advance a single step. The lesson I had learned through all my trials was to note, and never forget, that some have fallen further than others, and will not come back. To my own children I would say: Do not take the sympathy of others for granted. Do not presume they will respond as you do, or that they share your human compassion. To act without caution on such assumptions is to invite consequences as severe as death.

The lack of respect for immovable difference is the cause of endless human grief, and is why my father's dreams have failed.

After our descent from the mountains, April and I stopped in Santa Fe to visit my oldest childhood friend, Dan Wolfman. Danny and I were born a month apart in 1939 and had been passengers in the same baby carriage pushed by our mothers, who were also best friends. As infants we attended the same nursery school and remained close to each other until we left for colleges in distant cities. Now that our parents were gone, Danny Wolfman was the person I had known the longest who was still with me on this earth.

When I set up my first household in California and before I had any children, Dan and his wife, Marianne, stayed with us, spending the night in sleeping bags on the living-room floor in our one-bedroom apartment. It was 1960 and we were graduate students, all anticipating an endless horizon.

I was studying literature, while Dan had entered the field of archaeology, tunneling through time to retrieve the shards of lost civilizations. Over morning coffee he and Marianne talked enthusiastically about a dig they were headed for in Mesa Verde, where they intended to search the ruins of a cliff-dwelling tribe called the Anasazi, a Navajo word that meant "ancient people." More than a thousand years before, the Anasazi had carved stone pueblos in the side of a plateau rising out of Colorado's Montezuma Valley. Three hundred years after arriving, they abandoned the villages they had built and disappeared. Nobody knows where they went to or why; only their artifacts remain. Dan and Marianne were going to look for them.

Even in my imagination I had a hard time following their path. The very image of glacial time zones in which whole worlds were submerged was something I found oppressive. Perhaps I saw my own dreams swallowed up in mountains of indifferent earth alongside the Anasazi. While Dan and Marianne were looking backward in time, I was eagerly anticipating the revolutionary future. I couldn't begin to understand their romance with the long-buried past.

I lost touch with Dan for a long time after that, as we went our separate professional ways. For a time I lived in Europe, then returned to Berkeley to write. He got into the driver's seat of his Ford van, which was to be his transportation for the next thirty years, and took off on exotic travels into the heart of Mesoamerica. In Mexico and then in Machu Picchu, the lost city of the Incas, he would park his van and continue on horseback along wilderness trails, pursuing the lives of the ancient dead. Once, near Oaxaca, bandits posing as policemen kidnapped him and took his money and archaeological samples before releasing him unharmed. It was characteristic of his reticence that I never heard him refer to this adventure.

Eventually, Dan and Marianne settled in the state of Arkansas with their daughter, a beautiful child they named Lauren. He had been hired as the state archaeologist, and one of his projects was to take an inventory of the Buffalo National River. A generous teacher, Dan encouraged one of his students to develop a tree-ring chronology for the state and the entire Southeast, which had a significant influence on archaeological dating in the region.

When we were both in our forties, we met up again in our old neighborhood in New York. The physical change in him was noticeable and not only because his brown hair had acquired flecks of gray. There was an urgent appeal in his eyes and his complexion had turned a bright worrying red. Always a bear of a man, he had blown up to where the envelope of his body seemed about to explode. When he spoke, his voice was pinched as though his lungs were under pressure. I kept wanting to tell him to breathe.

The alarming appearance conveyed an equally disquieting reality. His doctors had detected an irregularity in his heart and his blood pressure was so high it had caused him to lose consciousness twice. He was just then recovering from a blow to the head suffered when he blacked out in the street and fell backward onto the pavement. Afterward, his doctors warned him to make changes in the way he conducted his life or face an early death. But it was evident that even under a sentence so dire he could not do it. My old friend Danny is going to die, I thought. We are only in our forties and in another ten years he won't be around.

I tried to talk to him and bring him back. With a feeling of immense futility, I urged him to stop what he was doing and change. Take deep breaths, I said, helplessly. *Slow down.* "But I can't," he replied. "There are things I *have* to do." I marveled how a man who inhabited time zones measured in eons could be so ensnared by the imperatives of a few weeks in the present. But he was. He had scientific rivals to respond to and positions he needed to defend. "I'm scheduled to give two important papers at a conference next month. I can't afford to miss the deadlines."

Dan was a pioneer in the specialized field of chronometrics, and was working on a specific technique for dating artifacts called archaeomagnetism. The earth, whirling through space, shifts its axis over the course of time and thus its magnetic pole. The shifts have been mapped. A hearth built by the Anasazi contains traces of iron in its clay floor. These traces are magnetized in a pattern that parallels the shifting positions of the earth's field. When the Anasazi fired the hearth more than a thousand years earlier, the pattern froze. By matching the magnetic lines in the ancient clay to the time map of the polar shifts, Dan could date the hearth itself.

Measuring these samples required a magnetometer and other lab equipment to which Dan had no access for most of his career. To secure lab time he had to travel to California, which added to his pressures, but also made it possible for me to see him. Recently he had obtained a job at the Museum of New Mexico in Santa Fe. He moved into a small adobe house in town, where he resided alone. Marianne had left along the way, and now lived a thousand miles distant on the West Coast, where their daughter, Lauren, was going to college.

Dan's museum position came with the promise of a new archaeomagnetic laboratory, which had been completed the year before April and I went to see him. On the road to Santa Fe, I looked forward to our meeting with anticipation. I was happy that I had been wrong and that he was still alive more than ten years after our encounter in New York.

At his suggestion, we met in a local breakfast café with oak tables that were warm from the autumn sun. The conversation over breakfast was bathed in the nostalgias of our own lost time. As we talked about his life in Santa Fe, I began to feel a pang of discomfort at having brought April with me, who was the very image of my own late-achieved happiness. It made me acutely conscious that he was alone and his health problems were still with him. He was overweight and his face was flushed. When I asked about his health, he said he was scheduled to go into the hospital the next month to have his heart fibrillated. There was no particular incident that made the medical procedure necessary, he added. It was just something his doctors ordered to be safe. Santa Fe was not a backwater, I reassured myself, and it would be a good hospital with doctors who knew what they were doing. I felt a deep affection for this man I had known longer than any other, and whom I could not help.

Near the end of the meal, I had occasion to go to the men's room and left April and Dan at the table. "When you were gone," she told me later, "he leaned over and asked me, 'How old are you?'" I told her I didn't think he intended disapproval by this question. I thought it was more like an encouragement to himself. April was thirty-three, which was twenty-two years younger than either of us.

April and I said our goodbyes to Dan and went back to California to resume our lives. A month later he went into the hospital, where they hooked him up to the fibrillation machine for the routine procedure. Soon after, I received a call from Marianne, whom I hadn't seen or heard from in thirty-four years, since she and Dan were students bedded down on my living-room floor.

"Dan is dead," she said. "He went into the hospital for the procedure and they lost him."

FIVE
Into the Future

TEN YEARS LATER, I AM STILL PUSHING ON. The universe I inhabit remains a mystery but I go on living and writing nonetheless, as though there were a reason for both. I have survived long enough to see my time map run in reverse. The future is now a dwindling proposition. If there are twenty years in front of me it will be enough to consider myself lucky.

Almost every day I create an order on the page, which reflects the order I see in the world. Whether it actually is one or not doesn't matter as much as the fact that the search moves me forward as though I am headed somewhere, and rescues me from the despair that would overwhelm me if I were not. In any case, I am so far along in my journey that there are projects I am reluctant to begin now, because I do not know whether there will be time enough to finish the page.

If I did not believe there was actually an order, I suppose I would not be able to pursue one at all. The quest is my comfort and the order my personal line of faith. They put oxygen into the air around me and allow me to breathe.

At the halfway mark of the last century, which to me does not seem so long ago, the gifted American writer William Faulkner won the Nobel Prize for Literature, an award, like every other human vanity, bestowed on the undeserving and the deserving alike. Faulkner titled his most famous novel, *The Sound and the Fury,* after a Shakespearean tragedy, *Macbeth*. Shakespeare's story is about a nobleman who in pursuit of worldly gain betrays every human value and relationship that is meaningful to him. In the process he is stripped of all human companionship and respect, until he is only an empty and embittered shell. "My life has fallen into the sere, the yellow leaf," he reflects. Having emptied his own life of its spiritual supports, he turns against life itself, which he describes as "a tale told by an idiot, full of sound and fury, signifying nothing."

When Faulkner mounted the podium in Oslo to receive his Nobel Prize and felt as though he was speaking to the world, he struck a very different note. The year was 1950, the dawn of the nuclear era. Faulkner looked into the eye of its darkest prospect and declared, "I refuse to accept this. I believe that ... when the last ding-dong of doom has clanged and faded ... in the last dying red evening ... man will not merely endure: he will prevail." Others criticized this pronouncement as mere bravado. What basis could Faulkner have to make such a claim? But this was not something he knew. It was his faith. It was the oxygen he needed to breathe.

April and I acquired a little Mexican dog with black and white markings, whose improbable name is Jacob and whose brain is smaller than my fist. When Jacob wags his tail to signal his happiness, he does not hide his pleasure as we who are burdened with consciousness sometimes do. Instead, his whole frame is swept into the motion as though life had no reality but this. Jacob is one of the myriad creatures on this earth, ridiculous and also beautiful, whose origin is a mystery and who do not worry the significance of who, or why, or what they are.

In the morning when I step out of my shower, this little self comes to me unbidden to lick the glistening drops from my feet. This is not a ritual of submission. It does not have any meaning for him at all. It is merely his pleasure. What is interesting is that I, a creature who lives by meanings, am also affected by this action. When he does not come, I feel the absence and miss him. This is a microcosm of all the visits and vacancies that bring joy and misery to our lives. Our choice is to embrace them or not. These are decisions we freely make that determine whether life will hollow us out and embitter us, or provide us oxygen to breathe.

Two years after my tumor was discovered, I went back to the Norris Cancer Center for an annual check. My first check six months after the operation had revealed a PSA level of 0.10—low for someone who still had a prostate, but apparently twice that for someone without one. I say "apparently" because like so much knowledge this too was uncertain. From a strictly scientific angle my fate remained a mystery. As do all.

For the next six months I lived with the possibility that some of the wilding cells might have leaked through the wall before the prostate was removed and then resisted the radiation afterward. When I took a second test, the level had dropped to where it was undetectable, indicating that I was disease-free. But now the number was up again, by one-half of one-tenth of a point— enough to be still tracking what might be a cancer, or not.

When I went in to consult Dr. Skinner about the result, he was his usual sanguine self. "We'll watch you. Even if it grows, the pace will be slow enough that more than likely you'll die of old age first. If it gets to a 5 or a 6, I'll order a bone scan. If it gets to 20, we'll probably give you some hormones to slow it down. But there's nothing to worry about. You'll probably die of natural causes before this gets serious."

I didn't understand the numbers. How could the 6 that I had registered when I first went to see him be dangerous enough to warrant an evisceration, but 20 not cause for alarm? How could the athletes I kept reading about in the news be given "three months to live," then push their cancers into remission and win gold medals? What was the secret of renewed life? What was *really* going on? I confronted Skinner: "If it's there, can't you just cut it out?" I said, even though I knew the answer. "There's nothing left to cut," he replied. "Come back in six months. We don't even know that this is a cancer. There's a difference of opinion over what such low postoperative levels mean. You'll probably live long enough to die of old age."

He conveyed these observations with a conviction that did not invite challenge. How would I challenge him anyway? Skinner's expression pre-empted such melodramas. He was a doctor, not a sorcerer. It occurred to me that this man had his own mortality to consider, and was closer to a natural span than I.

I had been alive for sixty-four years—not as long as Methuselah, but twice the age of Alexander. I was far enough along so that the cancer—if it was a cancer—would not make a hair of difference when it was over, just as Skinner said. I did not like the idea of carrying a time bomb inside me. But then who was not?

I had more symptoms of creeping age than any other malignancy. In fact, if I had a cancer—and it wasn't at all clear that I did—I had no symptoms at all.

I left Skinner's office with a refreshed perspective. Once I accepted my condition, I was in a position to appreciate its positive aspects. The ticking—whether it was cancer or merely life—made it easier to keep vital distinctions in view, never letting me forget that the space I occupied was finite, no matter how limitless my desires. "This is the monstruosity of love, lady," Shakespeare's incurable romantic Troilus observed: "the desire is boundless, the act a slave to limit." He might have made that life. The monstruosity of life.

When I think of Troilus's complaint, the words never fail to bring to mind my romantic father and all those who long for a world made whole and a life that will not let them down. It was the limitless boundaries of my father's desire that took away his freedom. The hunger for redemption swallowed him up and buried him alive. He was right, of course, that the world is broken—along with its beauty, goodness and truth. What he could not accept is that it cannot be otherwise. What he could not understand was that the glory is in the brokenness: that we do it and we do not submit.

The poet Wallace Stevens embraced his fate. "Death," he wrote, "is the mother of beauty." What he meant was that all our significances—whether it is love or nobility or art itself—are created by the ending. If there were no end, why would anything matter? If time is infinite, what is the moment? If nothing can be lost, what can be gained? Therefore, consider what you have and be grateful for it, and remember to look while your eyes are still open.

Isn't that just like you, to think you can psych out death by treating it as an aesthetic device? This could be my father's voice, but it is my friend Peter's. Years earlier he had become a devout Catholic. When he read my text and made this comment, it was Ash Wednesday, the beginning of Lent, the last suffering days of his Savior's time on earth.

My answer to Peter is this: I understand the finality of death, and do not make light of the end. But my journey has led me to these conclusions, which I cannot deny so late in its course. I have no faith in a life hereafter. But I will not be desperate over my own disappearance. If there is nothing further, what of it? Why should I waste my time left in misery over what I cannot change?

The voice I could not answer was April's. "You're so arrogant," she rebuked me. "Think of what God has done for you. Look at the times He has looked after you, how He saved you from cancer. You need to show some gratitude. I need you to do this for me. If you don't believe, you won't be there when I come for you and I'll be alone. And I don't want to be without you."

I tried to soothe her. "Don't fret," I said. "If there is a God, I am sure He is merciful, and will not condemn me for my lack of faith. Life cannot be merely a test to see if God's children will believe."

I thought this reasoning effective, but the pain in her eyes would not quit. She was already missing me.

Her distress caused me to reconsider what I had said. In fact, I had no answer. I *was* arrogant. If there was a God, how could I, in my mere mortality, know His plan? Maybe the whole idea was to see through the chaos and, through an act of faith, discover the divinity in it all. I had lived a charmed life, and had no explanation why. Once again I was forced to question what I had taken for granted and ask, *Is it I who is blind?*

"I'll think about it," I said.

"I don't want you to think," my wife replied. "I want you to open your heart."

In the afternoon light, April was golden. She was clutching the string of a heart-shaped party balloon whose metallic surface was painted with brightly colored flowers and the inscription, "I Love You Mom." It had been filled with helium and was straining at its tie.

"It's Mother's Day," April said. "I bought a balloon for your mother."

"My mother is dead."

"That's why I bought the balloon. To send it up to her, to keep her spirit alive. When it goes up to heaven, her spirit will grab hold of it."

I followed my wife onto the deck at the back of the house, facing the ocean. The afternoon sea was a cobalt blue, ruffling in the dry wind like goose flesh, as though its skin had come alive. I scrutinized the object she held with the eyes of a skeptic, just as my father would if he were still alive. What am I going to do with this toy, I thought, and how will I deal with these childlike fantasies?

But then I allowed myself to breathe and take in the moment. As I did so, I was pulled up into my wife's feeling for my absent mother and for her wounded son. I thought of the long-dead woman who had delivered me in pain into this world and watched over me as long as she was able. I recalled the years when age had overtaken and crippled her, and I had cared for her; I remembered back to when she was young and handsome and had taken time from her own pleasures and plans to look after me and set me on my way. And I missed her.

As I let my dead mother come near, I also let the corniness of the little object go. It seemed to me now a perfect symbol of our helplessness as we struggle to resist inexorable losses. It captured the feebleness with which we seek to express our hurt and the futility with which we scan the eternal silence in search of a help for our irreparable woes.

> *Oh Lord, when I consider the heavens,*
> *the work of your fingers, the moon and the*
> > *stars*
> *which you have set in their places,*
> *what is man that you are mindful of him,*
> *the son of man that you care for him?*

I cut the weight from the end of the string and the heart rose up. As it left my hand, April shouted after it, "We love you Blanche; we'll meet you in heaven." For moments I just stood watching the balloon dance skyward in the breeze, feeling the familiar pain of old memories. Then April turned to me and asked if I thought our little messenger would be able to reach my mother beyond the clouds, which now seemed impossibly high above us.

I had been wondering myself. I reflected on how our technological ingenuity had already lifted us over the top of the clouds; how I was used to traveling myself at altitudes high above the point where the plastic heart would finally give out and float gently back to earth. I was thinking: we already know too much for heaven. Our ancestors looked skyward and were humbled by its mystery and made reverent by its wonder. But we have been up there, and know what it is, and are convinced of what it is not. If by some chance my mother's spirit was out there, the little craft we had fashioned was not going to reach her.

But even as I thought this, I was aware of how liquid I had become, how the heartache I had suppressed for years had returned to the surface to remind me of what I had lost and how powerless I was to get it back. Even if the little heart would never make it to the lowliest cloud, it had already taken me to her; and for a moment her spirit, as April promised, was alive again.

My children and grandchildren are filling up the spaces I have left. It is through them that life comes to me now. They pull me toward it, and remind me that I am leaving. In my grandchildren I see the energies of my childhood and the horizon of expectation stretching endlessly in front of me. In their parents I watch myself gathering the next generation and hustling it forward to futures unknown. These are my rings of time. They remind me of who I was and am no more. Like the lost civilizations they tell me where I am going and where I have been. I feel my ancient-ness in them.

I know how I will leave. When my time comes, I will be engaged at full throttle, or the best I can muster. If I am fortunate I will be alert and April will be beside me and—if their busy lives permit—my children, and their children, and my stepson as well. Then a beat, and my soul will start ascending like my mother's heart. It will not dance slowly but go like a rocket to a destination unknown, perhaps to nowhere at all. And that doesn't bother me. If I allow myself regrets it is for the occasions I did not do what I should have, and for those when I failed to do what was right. It is for not being grateful enough.

For a time, my departed spirit will live on in others, especially April and my children and theirs, who will remember me and keep me in their hearts, until they too are gone. And then it will be over. But I won't feel cheated. Now or ever. I will not regret a moment that I lived to the full or did what was good. Nor will I regret the love I gave to my family and friends, or the kindnesses to strangers who deserved them. But then it will be done, and it will be left to others to fill in the spaces.

It will all happen so fast and so finally that one moment I'll be here, and the next I'll be gone.

Acknowledgment

I want to thank my publisher and friend Peter Collier, who has stood by this book as he has stood by me throughout my life.